The Sabbath

A thought for each day of the year

Philip M. Hudson

Copyright 2020 by Philip M. Hudson.

Published 2020.

Printed in the United States of America.

All rights reserved.

No portion of this book may be reproduced, stored in a retrieval system, or transmitted in any form or by any means – electronic, mechanical, photocopy, recording, scanning, or other – except for brief quotations in critical reviews or articles, without the prior written permission of the author.

ISBN 978-1-950647-31-6

Illustrations - Google Images.

This book may be ordered from online bookstores.

Publishing Services by BookCrafters
Parker, Colorado.
www.bookcrafters.net

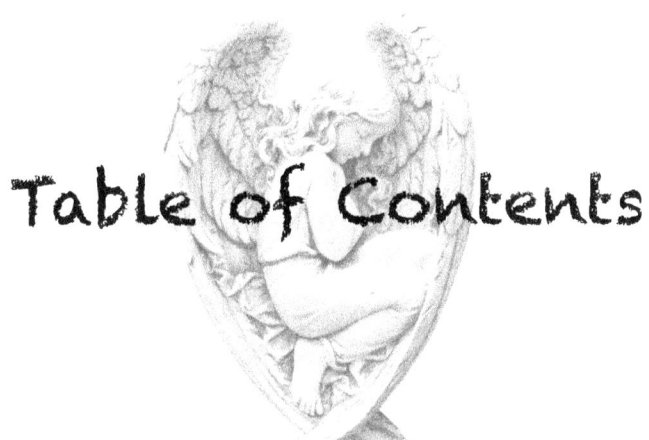

Table of Contents

Acknowledgements..i
Preface...v
Introduction..vii

A Thought For Each Day Of The Year...1
About The Author..367
By The Author..369
What More Can I Say?...373

The
Sabbath
can catalyze
our relationship
with God when it
shatters the icy grip
of our captivity to
Satan; and all is
because of the
Atonement
of Christ.

Acknowledgements

In this volume, I have attributed quotations to original authors whenever possible, as well as when I have editorialized their ideas. In many cases, however, my language will naturally reflect the teachings of leaders and members of The Church of Jesus Christ of Latter-day Saints.

The list of those who have contributed to this book is endless. As I have organized my own thoughts, I have realized how heavily I have borrowed from the towering examples of those who, over the years, have been my mystical mentors, my sensible chaperones, my spiritual guides, my surrogate saviors, my compassionate critics, and everything in between.

They are my avatars, manifestations of deity in bodily forms, my na'vi, the visionaries, who communicate with God on a level to which I can only aspire, and my tsaddik, whom I esteem as intuitive interpreters of biblical law and scripture. They are my divine teachers incarnate. They have offered listening ears, extended open arms, lifted my spirits, shown me the way, stretched my mind, reinforced my faith, strengthened my testimony, helped me to discover my wings, given immaterial support, provided of their means, emboldened me with words of encouragement, cheered me on with wise counsel, taught me humility, been there to steady me, soothed my troubled soul, stepped in to nurture me, led me to fountains of living water, wet my parched lips with inspired counsel, and bound up my wounds.

When I think of the influence of a multitude of angels thinly disguised as my family, friends, and peers, I remember the words of Sir Isaac Newton, who, when pressed to reveal the great secret behind his accomplishments, simply replied: "I stood on the shoulders of giants." Of course, at the end of the day, I alone am responsible for the content of this volume. But I hope my interpretations of principles and doctrine will cultivate your interest to dig deeper into the themes woven into this tapestry, by turning to the scriptures and seeking inspiration from the Spirit. My only goal is to help you to expand your insights into the telestial mile markers, the terrestrial truths, and the celestial guidelines that accompany each of us during our quest for enlightenment through our obedience to the Law of the Sabbath.

We are
sanctified by the
Law of the Sabbath.
Our "minds become single
to God, and the days will
come that (we) shall see him;
for he will unveil his face" unto
us. (D&C 88:68). We will no longer
be hobbled by limiting beliefs. "Now,
we see through a glass, darkly; but
then face to face; now (we) know
in part; but then shall (we) know
even as also (we are) known."
(1 Corinthinans 13:12).

It may come as
a shock, but for all
intents and purposes, we
are dead weight. It is thru the
Law of the Sabbath that we may
draw upon the Lord's strength to
carry us until we can walk without
becoming weary, and run without
fainting. We need the focus of
His energy on His holy day, if
we ever hope to gather His
stamina and use it as a
powerful force for
good, to disperse
the extra pounds
of darkness in
our lives.

Preface

I love to learn by reading the scriptures, and I often think of St. Hilary, who wrote in the third century: "Scripture consists not in what we read, but in what we understand." In each of the musings within this volume, I have consistently tried to find a scriptural foundation and a spiritual confirmation as I put my pen to paper.

I am continually reminded of Nephi's counsel to press forward with complete dedication and steadfastness, or confidence with a firm determination in Christ, having a perfect brightness of hope, or perfect faith, and charity, or a love of God and of all men. If we do this, feasting upon the word of Christ, or receiving strength and nourishment as we ponder the doctrines of the kingdom, and particularly those that relate to the Sabbath, and as we then endure to the end in righteousness, we shall have eternal life, which is the greatest of God's gifts. (See 2 Nephi 31:20).

It is with love, then, that I extend to you the invitation to enjoy this omnibus of random thoughts. Embrace it at face value, and use its observations relating to baptism as a springboard to your own personal plateaus of discovery, as you are taught by the Spirit to move in the direction of your dreams.

The Sabbath is a day of rest, but it is also the best time to bring us to a state of harmony with eternity. When our eye is single to the glory of God, we are liberated from confinement to the inexorable immutability of the laws governing our temporal world, and we are out and about, and busily involved in our Father's work and glory.

Introduction

If they are fortunate, novice quilters quickly learn a bit of wisdom from the Amish, who make some of the finest quilts in the world. On purpose, the Amish build mistakes into their projects, because they believe that any attempt on their part to design and produce a flawless creation would be a mockery of God, Who alone is perfect. The humility of the Amish makes me think of my own weak attempts to put the thoughts expressed in this omnibus to paper. In His infinite wisdom, God knows very well that I do not need to consciously plan on lacing my efforts with errors. That will come quite naturally, without the need for me to intentionally contribute to my short-comings.

Perhaps this serendipitous collection of musings will do little more than help to define quirks in my personality. Each of us is different, and many things, including our family and friends, the circumstances in which we find ourselves, the quality of our education, and our own personalities, inspire and mold our oral and written expressions. I would like to think that, in this text, all of these influences have been encouraging, affirmative, and constructive.

The reflections within this tome leave the door ajar for the reader, to allow shafts of the light of understanding to creep in. If, as I have expressed my thoughts, I mis-stated myself a few times, or flat-out got it wrong, I ask the patient indulgence and gentle correction of the reader.

Too often, I realize that my communications can be "carefully disguised with hypocrisy and glittering words," as Einstein put it. Although I do fancy myself a wordsmith, I have tried to avoid pedestrian expressions, idle language, and lazy scholarship. I do not pretend to be an authority on the Law of the Sabbath, inasmuch as I believe that we are all works in progress, but if you find the factual tone of a particular musing disengaging, the truth is that I typically experienced a deep personal involvement in my interpretation of the principles that illuminated its meaning.

In any event, when you open this volume, I hope you ponder these minute musings with as much enjoyment as I have experienced while creating them.

Without
the perspective
of our Sabbath day
instruction, we are more
likely to allow ourselves to be
caught up in the thick of thin things.
We tend to be short-sighted, and can be
insufferably self-indulgent, if only because
there are no parameters to help us establish a
foundation frame of reference, no standard to
which we may turn, no mentors to monitor our
progress, no Rod of Iron running straight and
true to which we may hold, no absolutes in
which we can confidently place a child
like trust, and no sustaining support
from a sympathetic priesthood.

It is within our Sabbath day instruction that we discover that "millions of candles can be lighted from a from a single flame, but the life of that first candle will never be shortened." (Buddha).

If
we allow
ourselves to
become isolated
from the sensitivity
to our surroundings
that is nurtured on the
Savior's Holy Sabbath,
may become inured
to our condition,
in the sense that
we are past
feeling.

Sabbath day teachings relating to our spiritual and physical health dictate that we will inherit our bodies in the resurrection. "The spirit and the body shall be reunited again in its perfect form; both limb and joint shall be restored to its proper frame." (Alma 11:43). Our spirits and our bodies must be kept equally pure and holy, in order for the Sabbath to bless our lives as envisioned by our Father in Heaven.

The instruction in Sabbath day school stands in sharp contrast to the short-lived pleasure in worldly ways that always evaporates as morning dew in the full light of day. Our obedience to our covenants alleviates the unfortunate consequences that must come into play when rebellion reaches "critical mass," as it surely must.

The Sabbath
binds us to heaven by
creating a pulsing stream
of inspiration whose flow has
has no temporal boundary and
no spatial limitation. Thru the
sacrifice of the Savior, and in
our worship services, we are
one with the mind and will
of our Heavenly Father.
Our hearts are knit
together in
love.

Since the
restoration of the
guiding principles that
are taught under priesthood
direction on the Sabbath day, the
knowledge of our origin and destiny
has been made available to all of the
children of our Heavenly Father. In other
words, in the Last Days, our sons and our
daughters shall prophesy, our young men
shall have visions, and our old men
shall dream dreams.
(See Joel 2:28).

To
paraphrase
the Apostle Paul:
Thanks be to God that
the Sabbath day has given
us the opportunity to lead
quiet and peaceful lives
in all godliness and
in all honesty.

If we open our hearts to the Holy Ghost, and allow ourselves to be molded through, His influence and by the Lord of the Sabbath, we can become holy and without spot.

If we
are too
busy to obey
the Law of the
Sabbath, it is likely
because we have become
absorbed in silly activities
that concentrate on obtaining,
accumulating, consolidating, and
securing our material interests. All
the while, however, the eternal
welfare of our souls hands
in the balance.

In our busy
and complex world,
we often see through a
glass darkly. This makes
it very difficult to discern
how to harness the power
of the elusive equations,
the majestic clockwork,
that is found within
the mathematics
of the Sabbath
day.

Our Sabbath day services are like a stethoscope that has the ability to detect our cardiac vital capacity. When our hearts have broken in contrition, the Master Physician is able to identify the steady sinus rhythm that will serve as His confirmation of congruence between our fallen nature and the atoning sacrifice of His only begotten Son, the Lamb slain from the foundation of the world.

Regard for the
Law of the Sabbath
gives us the chance to
catch a glimpse of heaven.
"Abundance is multiplied unto
(us) through the manifestations of
the Spirit" that are so profoundly felt
that they seem to overflow, as we realize
our righteous objectives. D&C 70:13). These
stay in focus because the spiritual guideposts
of our Sabbath day services provide us with an
orientation that is grounded on eternity. They
bless us with the only proven perspective in
a world that is overflowing with voices
that are in a fierce competition
for our attention.

The reach of the Atonement of Christ extends far enough to have power to neutralize the sins of the best of us and the worst of us. There is no beginning, nor is there a conclusion to its temporal and eternal influence. It only waits upon us to initialize its energy in Sabbath day worship services, to manifest its power, and to transport us into a state of harmony with the heavens.

In a coming day, when we come face to face with eternity, the spiritual element in which we find ourselves immersed will surely transform our mortal clay. Until that time comes, while we yet tarry upon the earth, we might ask ourselves under what circumstances does that element quicken us, and how can the pure knowledge that flows out of it be vitalized? Surely, it is "a man's wisdom (that will make) his face to shine, (and) the boldness of his face shall be changed." (Ecclesiastes 8:1). These miracles occur as we embrace the principles that are taught on the Sabbath day.

The direct frontal
assault by the adversary
on the divine principles that are
taught on the Sabbath, utilizes the
mutated forms of honor, truth, love,
goodwill, and virtue. These dreadful
distortions of character are made up
of bellicose behaviors, hostile habits,
cunning customs, recalcitrant rituals,
duplicitous deviations, sneaky social
conventions, insincere institutions,
as well as treacherous telestial
traditions. These fiery darts
can sabotage our best
efforts to embrace
the Law of the
Lord.

The more we
chase the worldly
caricatures of the peace
that can be ours when we
honor the Law of the Sabbath,
the more "the Right Stuff" will
elude us. However, if we plan our
work and work The Plan that finds
its expression on the Lord's holy day,
the happiness that has been prepared
for the Saints will come and rest
softly on our shoulders.

As we prayerfully
consider each element
of The Plan of Salvation
on the Sabbath, it seems that
our faith should remain fixed
on the revelations the Lord has
given us that relate to our world,
and not on mysteries that have not
been revealed to us, may never be
revealed, or that just may not
be pertinent to our current
circumstances.

The living water that spiritually sustains us on the Sabbath day of the Lord is the doctrine of the Gospel of Jesus Christ, including the covenant we make with God at the waters of baptism. Later, we symbolically renew that covenant in the ordinance of the Sacrament.

When our worship
has a foundation of
faith that is anchored to
the Lord of the Sabbath, we
are bound to Him Who has
sealed us His, and given
us the Spirit to be in
our hearts.

The sweet blessings of the Sabbath are within the reach of each of us, no matter what our cultural, social, political, economic, or religious situation might be. Principles that testify of its universal accessibility are supported by scriptures and are buttressed by Heavenly Father's declaration that He is no respecter of persons.

Those familiar
with the scripting of
the Three Act Play might
be aware of the Master's well
known reputation for theatrical
encore. Denigrators might see only
a frivolous repetition, or even look
in vain for even a brief intermission
from the Sabbath day's active and vital
engagement with life. However, sooner or
later, Heavenly Father will surely extend
an invitation to each of the participants
in the Play to have their moment in the
sun. Their minds will be illuminated by
the Light of Christ or the Holy Ghost.
In a spiritual awakening, they will
experience a confirmation of the
divine potential that had always
rested within their souls. They
will enthusiastically engage
the gentle reiteration of
the Sabbath day.

The principles of the
Great Plan of Salvation are
woven into the teachings of the
Sabbath curriculum. Without their
illumination, we would be doomed
to suffer in shadows where we would
experience only an indistinct flicker of
reality's illusions. The disparity between
the marginalized behavior of the worldly
and the ideals of the Law of the Sabbath
are readily apparent to the obedient,
and is addressed by the covenant
that is made in the ordinance
of the Sacrament.

Limiting beliefs
deafen us to mentors
who might otherwise help
us to monitor our progress.
They foster insensitivity to the
standards to which we might, in
other circumstances, turn. They can
corrode the iron rods running straight
and true that would have otherwise led
us to our Sabbath day services, and they
weaken our focus on the absolutes in
which the Comforter asks us to
place our implicit trust.

We will only be
able to feel the energy of
the Sabbath day after we have
warmed up our joints and tendons
with spiritually aerobic exercise, when
we have loosened up our ligaments through
compassionate service, when we have stretched
beyond our perceived capacity and have gained
the flexibility that comes with experience, when
we have worked out the 'nots' in our physical
and spiritual muscles by pushing ourselves to
our breaking point, when our vision can see
beyond our supposed limitations, and we
have raised our sights to fix our mind's
eye on a finish line that rises up to
meet a celestial horizon. Then,
when we have finally settled
in to a comfortable pace,
God will see us thru
to the end.

Heavenly Father
urges us to faithfully
attend our Sabbath day services
so that we may avoid the weeping
and wailing and gnashing of teeth
that accompany the recognition that
our days of probation are past because
we have procrastinated the day of our
salvation until it is everlastingly too
late, and our destruction is made
sure. (See Helaman 13:38).

When our hearts
are hardened against
the invitation that has been
extended by the Lord to repent,
it is as though our portion has been
diminished further and further, until
our defenses against the aggressive
tactics of the Devil crumble, and
we are left to fight our battles
alone, without the protection
that could have been ours,
had we observed to keep
the Law of the
Sabbath.

As we
come to the
conclusion of our
mortal journeys we
remember how it was the
Sabbath day that guided us
through the conceptual cul de
sacs, the doctrinal dead-ends, as
well as the telestial traffic jams that
always threatened to detour us from the
strait and narrow way. We will be forever
grateful for the Sabbath school that exposed
us to direct experience with the perfect law
of liberty, that permitted us to exchange the
uncertain course adopted by those who are
bound for the telestial kingdom, for the
celestial surety of exaltation in
the Kingdom of God.

The rational approach is doomed to failure and can never hope to plumb the depths of spiritual experience because it is grounded so firmly in the temporal world, relies so heavily upon the proofs of science, and requires the experimental confirmation of observable phenomena. Its logic is inherently self-defeating, because it denies the existence of the only power with the capacity to convey real understanding. This is why our Father in Heaven has initiated the Law of the Sabbath; to countermand the negative side of the opposition in all things, such darkness, error, pain, ignorance, evil, and misery.

Limiting beliefs exert enormous pressure on us to resist change and remain short-sighted; to become caught up in the moment, and continue in insufferable self-indulgence. They blind us to the frame of reference that is based on the unchanging principles that are often quietly revealed to us on the Sabbath.

In our Sabbath day services, we learn that our Heavenly Father is the Grand Architect of a divine design that establishes our familial roots and confirms His Fatherhood, that we might enjoy a witness that it is in Him alone that "we live, and move, and have our being; as certain also of (our) own poets have said. For we are also his offspring." (Acts 17:28).

Worship
on the Sabbath day
rounds out our weekly
experiences and portrays a
larger view of life. It smooths
out the rough edges that are created
as we bump and grind and lurch along
the rocky road of mortal life. It puts in
perspective our trials and tribulations, and
addresses the questions we never thought to
ask. It calms our troubled spirits, and
enables us to calmly comprehend the
rolling thunder of the mysteries
of the kingdom of God.

It is on the Sabbath
day, that we are taught
that our economic, physical,
and intellectual health have not
the power to save us, because what is
at stake is feeling, and not knowledge.
Only our spiritual well-being can come to
our rescue. As we begin the long journey of
discovery, our hearts and our nature will be
changed, as the scales fall from our eyes.
The path that lies before us will be best
illuminated if we retain the eye of
faith, so that we may see, with
an unobstructed view, all
the way into eternity.

We have been
foreordained in heaven,
even before the world was,
to have glory added upon our
heads forever, on the condition
of our faithfulness to God as we
support Him in His great work by
our actions. We are better able
to, so if we listen intently,
as Sabbath day worship
invites the Spirit into
our lives.

The Spirit
drives forward
the Kingdom of God
on earth. Those who bear
the priesthood do not focus
their attention on rituals that are
empty or passive. Rather, they exercise
their keys of authority to bless us with
the ordinances of the Sabbath in ways
that empower them to bind us to the
blessings of heaven by means of
covenants of action between
ourselves and the Lord.
In this way, everyone
is invested in the
endeavor.

When our minds
are locked on telestial
targets, and we even attempt
so-called higher level thinking
relating to the Law of the Sabbath,
without the influence of the Spirit,
we risk appearing as sounding brass
and tinkling cymbals. Without the
Holy Ghost, we are hollow on
the inside, and the echo of
silence is deafening
to the ears.

Because of the Law of the Sabbath, gratitude fills our hearts, as we think of the infinite Atonement of the Savior. We examine our lives through the magnifying glass of the Spirit to look for ways to improve. Because of the Sabbath day, we can fly higher than eagles, and He becomes the wind beneath our wings.

On the
Sabbath,
we recognize
that Jesus Christ
is the Son of God,
the Father of heaven
and earth, and is the
Creator of all things.
We honor His name,
and bear it with
respect and
reverence.

One of the miracles
of our Sabbath day worship
occurs as we burst free of the
dimly lighted corner of reality
where we had been living, that
afforded us only a limited
perspective that was
frozen in time.

If we really want to plumb the spiritual depths of the Sabbath day, and always have the Spirit to be with us, we need to experience how the Holy Ghost manifests personal revelation. "For God speaketh once, yea twice, yet man perceiveth it not. In a dream, in a vision of the night, when deep sleep falleth upon men, in slumberings upon the bed; then he openeth the ears of men, and sealeth their instruction." (Job 33:4-16).

Worship
on the Sabbath
generates repetitive
opportunities to smell
the delicious aroma of
the bread of life that has
been baking in a celestial
oven. In anticipation of a
buttered slice, we steadily
move along on the path
that carries us closer
to the threshold of
our heavenly
home.

What we call "coincidence" is often simply our Heavenly Father Who is working behind the scenes. Every moment on the Sabbath is influenced by His divine design. We need to be in tune with the Spirit, however, to recognize it and act upon it.

When we attempt
to subvert the elements
of The Plan by turning away
our faces from the Sabbath Law,
by engaging in destabilizing and
futile efforts to obtain opportunities
that our actions do not merit, and
by attempting to retain blessings
we do not deserve, we will be
rewarded with a pyrrhic
victory, at best.

We can better
relate to the other
participants in life's
Three Act Play, and they
to us, if we see each other
against the milieu of the First,
Second, and Third Acts, namely,
our pre-earth life, mortality, and
life after death. Knowledge of this
sweeping panorama, of the intricacy,
complexity, and sophistication of the
Play itself, is explained and reiterated
by the Spirit during the elements of
our Sabbath day worship services.

Nothing stifles the guiding Spirit faster than the stubborn self-confidence that has mutated into vanity, unbridled pride, selfishness, and haughtiness. These are the character crippling traits that are antithetical to the expansion of understanding that is found in the revelatory atmosphere of our Sabbath day services.

Every time we think
in rational terms, we hedge
ourselves in by the very things from
which we yearn to be free: our mortal
perspective and perceptions, that are, sad
it may seem, the sum and substance of our
temporal experiences. Because of the Light
of Christ, we all intuitively seek the right
answers, but if the Sabbath doesn't lead
us to enlightenment, we are doomed
to ask the wrong questions, and
to do so habitually.

One
of the terrible
consequences of the
world's fascination with
Babylon, and of its adoption
of the lifestyle of Beelzebub, is
spiritual insensitivity that is born
of competition between individuals.
Win or lose is the prevailing standard.
Zero sum game is the rule of play. While
business teaches that we don't get what we
deserve; we get what we negotiate, on the
Sabbath day we realize that appeasement,
mediation, concession, compromise, and
arbitration are conspicuously absent.
We see only the work and glory
of God in action, which is a
win-win for everyone

Sabbath
day observances
soften our telestial
tendencies and create
an impenetrable shield of
faith. The Plan of Salvation,
of which they testify, provides a
sounding board against which we
may assess the polarized opposites
that seek our attention. The center of
our worship, which is in the Atonement,
describes the differences between joy
and its worldly counterfeits. As we
obey the Law of the Sabbath, we
can feel familiar chords that
are struck within our
heartstrings.

The Sabbath can catalyze our relationship with God when it shatters the icy grip of our captivity to Satan; and all is because of the Atonement of Christ.

No form of government, and no level of material well-being will save us, to paraphrase Abba Eban. Our salvation will be possible only when towers fall and Jerusalem finally triumphs over Babylon. What is at stake, then, is not only intelligence, but also feeling. We have to change our hearts. Redemption, according to the prophets, is preconditioned by our repentance, which leads the faithful to honor the Lord on the Sabbath.

In between
the sights and
sounds, rides and
attractions, and thrills
and spills of our earthly
theme-park experience, the
Sabbath day teaches us how to
use spiritual hygiene practices
to remove the grit and grime
that accumulates as a part of
life, but that always threaten
to foul our inner workings
and curtail our progress
on the pathway toward
perfection.

Since
everything has its
opposite, even as there
is faith, so must there also
be its worldly counterpart. In
our day, the grip of fear paralyzes
many of God's children. Today, more
than ever, we need the Sabbath day. We
need the assurance of peace, that our
lives are moving in the direction of
our dreams, and that it is thru the
Atonement that we are given the
tools we all need to hitch our
wagons to the stars in the
heavens that trace the
pathway to glory.

Those who
settle for the moral
mediocrity of character
crippling personality flaws
can never get enough of what
they don't need, because what
they don't need will never
satisfy them. Whether they
know it or not, what
they do need is the
Sabbath day in
their lives.

Our Sabbath day worship services, and the Atonement of Christ, have worked their magic when the Spirit of the Lord falls upon us, and we are filled with joy. When we are clean, we enjoy a peace of conscience that defies any explanation, except the obvious ones.

Our
observance of
the Law of the Sabbath
has the potential to order
our chaotic world, to bless us
with clarity rather than confusion,
to teach us how to achieve fluency in
the language of the Spirit, as well as to
educate those who remain functionally
illiterate, speaking of their Gospel
scholarship, so that all might be
equally mesmerized by the
reason for the Sabbath
day and its season
of joy.

The
doctrine that
is taught in our
Sabbath day services is
sometimes just a shadow
of that which is yet to come,
and it cannot be understood at
anywhere near the level of God's
comprehension. As Paul wrote: "For
now we see through a glass, darkly;
but then face to face: now I know
in part; but then shall I know
even as also I am known."
(1 Corinthians 13:12).

"Spirits can only be revealed in flaming fire and glory." (Joseph Smith, "Times & Seasons," 4:331). Paul wrote that God can be best described as "a consuming fire" in the sense that His Presence, His glory, is akin to fire, smoke and everlasting burnings. The hours spent in Sabbath day services remind us that time is the fire in which we burn. They prepare us for that day when He will reveal Himself, unveil the heavens, and divine fire fills all the earth; when the elements of our world melt, and the mountains flow as rivers; when valleys will be exalted, and all rough places will be made smooth.

On the Sabbath, we sometimes have a striking experience when light, or truth, gradually distils upon our souls. Just so, in the Sacred Grove, light "descended gradually," entering the quiet grove slowly enough that Joseph was able to gauge its approach until it finally reached him and enveloped him within a dazzling brilliance. It was only then that he "saw two Personages, whose brightness and glory (were beyond all) description," and who stood suspended in the air within the encircling light. (J.S.H. 1:17). We may not see Them, but on the Sabbath day, when we are personally inspired here a little, and there a little, we can be sure that we are in our own sacred grove.

The law
of the Sabbath is
life-generating and it is
life-sustaining, for just as we
are "born into the world by water,
and blood, and the spirit" and have
become of dust living souls, even so, we
"must be born again into the kingdom of
heaven, of water, and of the Spirit, and
be cleansed by blood," even the blood
of the Son of God, and receive our
instruction on the Sabbath, that we
"might be sanctified from all sin,
and enjoy the words of eternal
life in this world, and eternal
life in the world to come,
even immortal glory."
(Moses 6:59-60).

Ward and
stake sanctuaries
are constructed out of
the best and the sturdiest
materials, to withstand the tests
of both time and circumstance. The
leaders of the Church are well aware
of Hosea's terrifying caution that when
the world sows the wind, it can expect
to reap the whirlwind. Therefore, the
edifices that house our Sabbath day
observances have been designed to
withstand the worst that the devil
can muster, as the destruction
that was foretold sweeps
across the landscapes
of our lives. (See
Hosea 8:7).

As we embrace the
power of the Holy Sabbath,
we are blessed with visions
of the Celestial Kingdom that
dance before our eyes. Our faith
in the Savior moves us closer to
heaven's gate. We first seek the
kingdom and His righteousness.
We have learned that when our
priorities are guided by the
Spirit, we need not fear
for want of our most
basic needs.

We cannot expect the
Law of the Sabbath to deliver us
from consequences. It provides no
protection from poor choices, shows
no leniency to those who have allowed
themselves to be mesmerized by mediocre
philosophies, and it permits no justification
for rationalization. Those who only desire
theological titillation, and refuse to be
taught by the Spirit, will find little to
interest them as they clumsily tread
upon the sacred ground of the
Sabbath day of the Lord.

A simple yet uncommitted recognition of Jesus Christ will not qualify us to inherit the Celestial Kingdom. Christians of convenience lack the fire that is ignited by Sabbath day worship. Many honorable people who accept the Lord will still inherit the Terrestrial Kingdom. According to the scriptures, these are they who "received not the Gospel, neither the testimony of Jesus, neither the prophets, neither the everlasting covenant. Last of all, these are all they who will not gather with the Saints, to be caught up unto the Church of the Firstborn, and received into the cloud." (D&C 76:101-102).

On the
Sabbath, that
is the holy day
of the Lord, we are
cast off from the self
limiting conditions and
self defeating behaviors that
would otherwise have blinded
us to a larger view of life. We
enjoy a settled conviction of
the truth. That peace follows
our obedience to celestial
principles that are taught
in Sabbath school and
that brings His Rest
within reach of
our uplifted
hands.

That
which we
undertake to
accomplish on
the Sabbath stands
as a witness that we
may take God at His
word when He declares
that it is His work and
glory to bring to pass
our immortality and
eternal life.

Our finest hour is the time spent
in Sabbath school, when unexpected
challenges are met with extraordinary
efforts. Just like the Seven Dwarfs, when we
embrace the tenets of the Gospel, we whistle
while we work out our salvation, because of
the miracle of the Atonement. We learn how
our Heavenly Father has linked our own
efforts to those of His Son. Happiness,
as it turns out, is the object and
design of our existence, and it
will be the end thereof, if
we follow the path of
repentance that
leads to
it.

When
we are born
again and we
participate in the
ordinances of the
Gospel as members
of the Church, we find
that we oriented more to
the expansive laws of the
hidden world of eternity,
and less to the restrictive
confines of our physical
surroundings. Thus, we
find that our spirits
are nurtured thru
Sabbath day
services.

A wonderful benefit of our Sabbath day worship services is that after our participation in the ordinance of the Sacrament, we will receive the strength to endure the suffering that is part of life, but that is not of our own doing. As we bear the strips of the world, we will abound in the patience of faith.

The brilliantly crafted Sabbath day of worship has been designed as a celestial thermostat that easily mitigates the volatility of the telestial tempests that regularly sweep across our lives.

As we
come to our
Sabbath day services
with questions that have
been on our minds, we find
ourselves poised at the edge of
forever. We jump off into a stream
of revelation, to be carried along
in a quickening current that we
recognize is no less than direct
experience with God. In our
interaction with the Saints,
we find divine guidance
to take our bearings
on eternity.

The Plan, God knew
that, with only nine months
to put the final touches on our
preparation, we would transition
from the eternal world where we had
enjoyed the warmth of hearth and home
in heaven, to the bleak atmosphere of the
lone and dreary world here on earth. When
we did so, He knew that there would be an
immediate disconnect that would be both
brutal and unrelenting in intensity. That
disengagement makes it imperative that
we find our way to the holy sanctuaries
that He has commanded must be built
to shelter the tens of thousands of
the congregations of Saints, on
the Sabbath day of the Lord.

The fire that was kindled on Sinai burned all the way from the earth "unto the midst of heaven" itself. (Deuteronomy 4:11). Moses, who witnessed this manifestation, thought he could see through a brilliant conduit, as it were, right into eternity. So it is, during services on the day of the Lord.

Within the Law of the Sabbath is the teaching that it is only those who passionately embrace the Gospel with its ordinances and covenants who will go to the highest degrees of glory to live in the presence of the Gods. "These are they who are priests and kings, who have received of his fullness, and of his glory; and are priests of the Most High, after the order of Melchizedek, which was after the the order of Enoch, which was after the order of the Only Begotten Son. Wherefore, as it is written, they are (as the) gods, even the sons of God." (D&C 76:56-58).

The faithful
need not fear,
although they "see
signs and wonders, for
they shall be shown forth
in the heavens above, and in
the earth beneath. And they shall
behold blood, and fire, and vapors
of smoke." (D&C 45:40-41). Although
the spiritual equivalents of lightning
may strike all around them, they
will be shielded from harm by
the copper grid of the Sabbath
that surrounds them and
that grounds them to
the Savior.

Without
the influence
of the Sabbath,
our hearts are too
easily set upon worldly
possessions. Our spirituality
is homogenized until we no
longer look forward to worship
as our habitual routine. We settle
for an economy hotel room, having
dismissed from our minds the four-star
all-inclusive world class accommodation
that continues to extend its invitation from
just beyond the parted veil of our covenant
of baptism. The only resort fee that we
need to pay in order to reclaim the
delights of the Sabbath day is that
of clean hands and a
pure heart.

The foundation of the
Sabbath is planted on bedrock,
as was the wall that was built by
an Irishman around his farm. Asked
why he made it five feet high and eight
feet wide, he replied that if the wind ever
blew so hard that it toppled the wall, it
would still be five feet thick. There is
a redundancy that is built into our
Sabbath day observance, and in
its repetition we are protected
by a shield of faith that is,
for us, at least five
feet wide.

The ability of the Sabbath day to order our chaotic world, and to bless our lives with clarity rather than confusion, to simply teach us how to be fluent in the language of the Spirit, is mind boggling.

"I had rather be a doorkeeper in the house of my God, than to dwell in the tents of wickedness." (Psalms 84:10). On the Sabbath day, we bloom where we are planted; we serve where we have been asked to do so.

Even when we
take an active part in
worship on the Sabbath, we
cannot hope to chart the
unknown possibilities of
existence until we have
recognized our moral
obligations as both
transcendent
and divine.

It is
our Father's
desire for each
of us to satisfy the
entrance requirements
for admittance into the
inner sanctum on the holy
day of rest. God could not
bless us with a greater gift
to do so, than that of the
Spirit, Who will teach us
the mysteries of the
kingdom, on the
Sabbath day of
the Lord.

We honor
the Sabbath of
the Lord, because
we do not want to
be spiritually starved,
doctrinally dehydrated,
or intellectually inhibited
while only inches away from
the living bread that could
have satisfied our hunger,
or from the fountains of
living water that could
have slaked our thirst
or even healed us of
our sins and our
blemishes.

The great and
eternal purposes of
our Father in Heaven,
Whose plans are vividly
articulated in Sabbath day
services, were prepared from
before the foundation of
the world.

The knowledge
of our divine heritage
that is clearly taught in
our Sabbath schools acts as
a catalyst, inspiring us to be
at our very best. The Sabbath
invites us to brush up against
the face of God. It gentles
our condition.

As
we hone
our revelatory
capabilities, we can
build upon experiences
with the Spirit that we have
already had, that include our
testimonies of the Law of the
Sabbath, of the endowment,
and of the other rites and
ordinances of the House
of the Lord.

When we obey the Law
of the Lord on the Sabbath
day, we will find that we have
come home to a more comfortable
and a more expansive dominion,
where both power and authority
take on new meanings that
were beforehand only
dimly perceived.

The
Sabbath
provides the
loom upon which
we busily weave the
complex tapestry of our
lives, as we create our own
coats of many colors. But central
to the vitalization and execution of
our efforts is detailed instruction that
comes from above, in the form of
personalized guidance from the
Master Tailor Himself, as well
as from His ordained
apprentices.

The enthusiastically ignorant attempt to drag communication from the heavens down to their level so that it is in harmony with their myopic view of life. The world ridicules revelation, disparages its delivery, and cannot comprehend why the faithful would obey the Law of the Sabbath or pay obeisance to an unknowable god. Their ineffectual remonstrations ring hollow, when compared to the thunder, the lightning, and the burning bush on Sinai.

We take for granted
that the prophets and seers
among us receive revelation.
But isn't it wonderful when the
sound of the voice of the Lord
that is so familiar to them is
for us a continuous melody
and a thunderous appeal,
as we worship on the
Sabbath day?

If we have
faith in the atoning
power of Christ, and if
we furthermore possess the
resolve to do whatever we must
do to initiate the spiritual energy
that is lying dormant within us, we
will profit by the administration
of ordinances on the Sabbath.
Ultimately, these will lead
us to the blessings of
the House of the
Lord.

The way to
comprehend the hidden
treasures of knowledge that
are woven within the Sabbath, is
by pressing forward with dedication
to feast upon the words of Christ. We
thereby receive the physical and spiritual
strength and nourishment that we need
in order to righteously endure to the
end with continuing responsibility
and accountability, benevolently
supported at all times by the
sustaining influence of
the Spirit.

The
Sabbath day
encourages us to
vividly role-play, as
well as to pre-play and
re-play the lines we have been
asked to deliver in the theater of
life. It gives us the tools we need to
be the poor understudies to the Star
of the production, our Headliner,
Who is our Lord and Savior,
Jesus Christ.

Even Latter day Saints who faithfully embrace the Sabbath day of the Lord, may still ask, as did Moses: "Tell me, I pray thee, why are these things so?" The Lord hinted at the answer, when He declared that it was His work and glory to bring to pass our "immortality and eternal life." (Moses 1:30 & 39).

The Sabbath prepares us
to expose the evil designs of
those who would conspire against
us in the Last Days. We will not do
this "with railing accusation, neither
with boasting nor rejoicing," but instead
with the measured response one would
expect of the Lord's anointed, that is
characteristic of those who have the
confidence to walk in the light
of the Lord. (D&C 50:33).

The Law of the
Sabbath asks us to examine
how we have embraced the moral
element of responsibility that goes hand
in hand with knowledge. Do we possess the
spiritual and intellectual maturity to handle
knowledge with accountability? When we dare
to grapple with such interrogatives, we come
to an epiphany, as we determine to do our
best to be righteous stewards of the power
that has been given to us to honor
the Lord on His Sabbath day.

The Prophet Joseph Smith stated: "There are but a very few beings in the world who understand rightly the nature of God, and if they do not understand the character of God they do not comprehend themselves." (H.C. 6:303). The purpose of our obedience to the laws of the Gospel that relate to the Sabbath is to help us to develop the qualities and the character traits of our Father, that will be consistent, through our faith, with His divine nature.

Those
who obey
the Law of the
Sabbath have learned
by personal experience
that the greatest miracle
is not raising the physically
dead, but healing the spiritually
sick. A hand picked trauma team
with specialty training in advanced
spiritual life support techniques
attends to the needs of those
who honor the Sabbath by
their attendance at
meetings.

Our Sabbath day
worship can launch us
into a profoundly personal
spiritual comprehension, when it
is built upon the foundation of the
connections that we have already made
with our Heavenly Father. When that happens,
we find ourselves about to be caught up into
the third heaven, poised to take a leap of
faith off the edge of forever, into
the bosom of eternity.

To maintain
the momentum that
has been generated during
our Sabbath day worship, and
in order to make it enduring,
new and established members of
the Church need to have sustaining
spiritual experiences. As Gordon B.
Hinckley said, every member of
Church, and particularly new
members, needs a friend, a
responsibility, and the
nurturing influence
of the good word
of God.

Our worship on the Sabbath day spawns creativity. Our innovation can be incremental or revolutionary, but its end result is always revelatory. The trickle-down economics of originality during our Sabbath day services increases value. The focus of our attention is not only on the end point, but also on the process. We are invited to enjoy the journey as much as we are prepared to anticipate the destination. The paradox is that all good things come only to those who patiently wait upon the Lord.

Our faith
in the divine Plan
of our Father in Heaven
is confirmed on the Sabbath,
when we learn that it has been
designed to bring us back into His
kingdom after we have grown up unto
the Lord, have spiritually matured,
and have learned that the basis
of our hope of salvation is
in His Atonement.

The Sabbath day has the depth, breadth, majesty, and capacity to encircle all of our Heavenly Father's children within His warm embrace. As the poet wrote: "He scribed a circle that drew me out. Heretic, rebel, a thing to flout! But (God) and I had the will to win. We scribed a circle that drew him in." (Edwin Markham).

The
teachings
of the Sabbath
soften our telestial
tendencies and create
an impenetrable shield of
faith. The Plan of Salvation,
of which it testifies, provides a
sounding board against which we
can discern between the polarized
opposites that seek our attention.
The Atonement, which lies at its
center, describes the difference
between joy and its worldly
counterfeits, and strikes
familiar chords within
our heartstrings.

Without the longitudinal perspective that we would have received by worshipping God on the Sabbath day, we must be ever learning but never coming to a knowledge of the truth. We grasp at straws, failing to recognize that nothing will keep us out of Zion more surely than the self-assurance that cannot acknowledge the influence of powers that are greater than ourselves. Nothing will kill the influence of the Spirit faster than absolute self confidence that too easily mutates into unbridled pride, selfishness, vanity, and haughtiness.

The Sabbath predisposes us to become all that God is, by teaching how to incorporate His image and likeness into our own being and nature. For our instruction to fulfil His promises, we must care for the earthly tabernacles of our celestial spirits. It is only in the Atonement that we find a way for our corruptible bodies to become clean and pure, and full of light.

Sabbath
day instruction
plots safe passage
through the minefields
of mortality. It documents
potential perils and pitfalls,
charts the recommended route
that leads to refuge, maps out
the success strategies we need
to follow if we wish to live
abundantly, and measures
our progress on the path
to perfection.

The way to the Sabbath school follows a road that not many travel. As the poet Robert Frost mused: "I shall be telling this with a sigh somewhere ages and ages hence: Two roads diverged in a wood, and I, I took the one less traveled by, and that has made all the difference.

If we hunger
and thirst to have
a comprehension of
principles and canon,
and approach our Sabbath
day worship anticipating a
spiritual feast, the doctrine
of the priesthood will distill
upon our souls as dews from
heaven, the Holy Ghost will be
our constant companion, and
by its power we may discern
the truth of all things.

Applying the things we learn at our Sabbath day services is the spiritual counterpart to dusting for dirty fingerprints on the idols with which Satan teases, taunts, torments, tempts, and tortures us. When we are negligent in Gospel scholarship, it is easier for the Devil to twist our focus inward.

The Law of the Sabbath releases our energies to be creative and fosters creativity, that we might experience a greater capacity. Its design is the perfect law of liberty. Our eternal welfare is thoroughly invested in the Sabbath. President Spencer W. Kimball recognized its nurturing potential when he urged us to lengthen our stride. Our worship on the Sabbath day will bless us with an awakening sensitivity that puts us in touch with our divine destiny.

If we do not rely upon the light-generating capacity of the Sabbath, we are doomed to dance about in flickering shadows that illuminate nothing but the caricatures of reality. The blind will stumble about in the dark until the discrepancy between their marginalized behavior and the ideals of the Sabbath day becomes so great that their short-lived pleasure in worldly ways will evaporate as the morning dew in the full light of day.

Although
we cannot save
our daylight time, we
may try to maximize it
by strangling ourselves with
what we can buy, things whose
opacity obstructs our ability to see
what is really there. In reality, we
are on Sabbath time. What we enjoy
is the Lord's time. We are on His
errand, no matter how long it
takes, or how preoccupied by
trivial concerns we
might be.

The Law of the Sabbath introduces us to self-shaping, self-supporting, self-sustaining and self-renewing behaviors. At its very core, its doctrine becomes a perfectly liberating law that allows us to reach our potential in an atmosphere of mutually supportive inter-dependency with the Savior. His work and glory become our quest for the holy grail of immortality and eternal life in the Celestial Kingdom.

Nothing can ever
make up for the dogged
discipline that is a prominent
trait of those who obey the Law
of the Sabbath. Cheap thrills will not
replace its lofty rewards, and novelty
and spectacle cannot defeat, but only
delay, implementation of its principles.
The universal influence of the Light of
Christ encourages us to set our sights
on the brightly burning beacon of the
the Holy Ghost, Who is waiting to
guide us in the company of the
Atonement across an ocean
of light to the discovery.
of a new world.

Each of us
pays dearly for
our secular education,
and we expect a return on
our investment. Our introduction
to Sabbath instruction is equivalent
to engaging in an independent study
fine arts program. Its requirements for
admission are simply a ready heart and
a willing mind, and there is no temporal
tuition. Its design and its purpose is to
teach us what we need to know and
do, that God may guide us back to
His heavenly home, to live and
love with Him in His kingdom.
Each week, on the Sabbath,
we receive confirmation
that He has left the
porchlight on
for us.

The
Sabbath
stands as a
solemn witness
of just how we will
behave if we are left
to our own devices, after
having received instruction
regarding what we should do.
Jesus Christ is the Architect of
the Cosmos, and those with the
mighty faith to obey the Law
of the Sabbath add strength
to His pillars of creation
each time they enter
the sanctuary of
His house.

Possibly the most significant difference that accounts for the superiority of obedience to the Law of the Sabbath over other behavioral lifestyle choices is the process whereby the Gospel of Jesus Christ is internalized by His disciples. The wonder of our transformation begins with sanctification by the Spirit at the waters of baptism, and reaches its zenith when we participate in the ordinances of exaltation that are carried out before holy altars in the House of the Lord.

Just two hours
of formal worship on
the Sabbath prepares us
for that moment when time,
as we understand it, will lose
all meaning. We appreciate that
"See you later," will no longer be a
part of our vocabulary. Time, that was
so often seen as a predator that stalked
us all of our lives, will in a coming day
be fondly remembered as a companion
that accompanied us on our journey
through mortality, reminding us to
cherish every moment.

When we
finally embrace
the Law of the Sabbath,
we will better understand
the experience of the people of
Zarahemla after the crucifixion of
the Lord. From the unseen world, "there
was a voice heard among all the inhabitants
of the earth, upon all the face" of the land. (3
Nephi 9:1). It was not a deafening voice of a
hundred decibels, but simply a quiet sound
that was heard by everyone regardless of
their temporal surroundings. It was a
voice quite unlike any sound that
had ever been heard, and it came
from immortal lips that would
have a profound effect on
both the heavens and
the earth.

To those who have prepared themselves by obeying God's Law of the Sabbath, the Lord "will shew wonders in the heavens and in the earth, (with) blood, and fire and pillars of smoke." (Joel 2:30). When He revealed Himself to Isaiah, His appearance was so commanding that "the posts of the doors moved at the voice of him that cried, and the house was filled with smoke. Then, (said Isaiah), Woe is me! For I am undone." (Isaiah 6:4-5). His physical frame could barely tolerate God's manifestation. He would need health in his navel and marrow in his bones, as well as strength in his loins and in his sinews, if he ever hoped to be successfully welcomed into the great and terrible presence of the Lord Himself. (See D&C 89:18, Proverbs 3:8, & Job 40:16).

We will all be tested by trials and temptations, and we will make mistakes. But we will rise above our failures because of the love of the Savior and His Atonement. It is in the next act that all the mysteries will be solved, all the pieces of the puzzle will be put in their proper place, all the confusion that sometimes tormented us will put to rest, and everything will be made right. If that is to occur, we need to be up and about starting now, by making our way to our Sabbath day worship services.

It is in
our classroom
instruction on the
Sabbath Day that we learn
that the world gauges success
using artificial measurements. But it
also powerfully teaches us that we come
from a more noble realm in which we were
taught that accomplishment is determined by
the building of character, and by rendering
service. As we engage the Law of the Sabbath,
we discover that religious recognition is
just that, a re-cognition or re-knowing
of the principles of provident living
that touch our spirits because they
are inherently treasured, true,
and trustworthy, inasmuch
as they come from
heaven.

Whenever, wherever, and however we fit into the cosmos, we do know this: God quickens life by providing us with the animation of the Sabbath day within which we freely interact with each other and with heaven. He "lends (us our) breath, that (we) may live and move and do, according to (our) own will, and (He supports us) from one moment to another." (Mosiah 2:21).

The
day is not
far off when our
mortal bodies must
put on immortality. This
may be accomplished as our
Heavenly Father carries us into
the greater dawn of heaven. Just as
ultraviolet light is used in sterilization,
(ultraviolet germicidal irradiation - UVGI),
could it be that it is the physical phenomenon
of the unearthly light that is intrinsic to God
that purifies and renews our sin-stained souls?
Perhaps the Law of the Sabbath has something
to do with the change that will come over
us, when our sins that had been as scarlet,
"shall be as white as snow; though they
(had been) red like crimson, they
shall be as wool."

Without the
perspective that the Sabbath
gives to us, our comprehension
of the observable universe is at risk,
because it is all too easy to set our sights
too low and edge into conceptual cul-de-sacs
from which there is no retreat. If we ignore its
perspective, we risk sliding backward into a
one-dimensional view of the cosmos where
we see things not as they really are, and
not as our Heavenly Father seems
them, but only as our limited
vision permits us to
see them.

When we stand before
the Bar of Justice, we will
acknowledge that the principles we
studied in Sabbath day school were not
haphazard or arbitrary, with corollaries,
footnotes, addenda, and exceptions to the
rule. Our obedience required neither analysis
nor interpretation by legal counsel, and our
accounting demanded no interpretation by
an expensive C.P.A.. These doctrines have
been clearly established and carefully
clarified with purposeful precision so
that there can be no disputation
concerning their accessibility,
applicability, and validity.
They are striking in
their simplicity.

As
we look
around at a
world that seems
to have gone mad,
the Sabbath stands as
a light that has been set
on a hill; an island in the
storm providing refuge from
the uncertainties and vagaries
of life. It speaks a language
of stability, direction, and
purpose to those who are
afraid, uncertain, and
hesitant in their
faith.

Those who attend their Sabbath day services are "strangers from a realm of light, who have forgotten all. And so, they must learn why they're here, and who they really are." (Doug Stewart). When we commune with the Saints in the household of faith, the memory of our former lives and the purpose of our call is awakened within our hearts. This sets the stage for us to travel a path along the second mile of faith to the stability of Gospel centered lives.

In our
Sabbath day
worship services, we
interact with members
of the Church who grapple
with their own custom-tailored
challenges, but who have somehow
made the transition from hesitancy to
conviction, from instability to commitment,
from timidity to confidence, from indecision
to resolution, from doubt to certainty, from
struggle to celebration, and from vacillation
to determination They have moved beyond
an indefensible spiritual itinerancy to
the moral discipline of faith.

It is primarily
because of the ever-present
threat of behavioral instability
that Heavenly Father has provided
us with the Law of the Sabbath. Therein
lies the power of obedience to reorient
us to righteousness, and to recalibrate
our moral compass so that it might
safely guide us home to the
happiness that has been
prepared for the
Saints.

For it
to function
in our lives, the
Law of the Sabbath
requires that we take
God's labor of love and
somehow ease onto a world
stage that is lit only by fire.
As we honor the Sabbath day,
we can amplify our yearning to
reach the most holy faith that was
envisioned by Heavenly Father, that
a comfortable connection with the
Holy Ghost might be created, as
well as a relationship with
heaven itself.

Families that worship together on the Sabbath provide the mortar that holds the parapets of the Celestial Kingdom together. Family grounds us to mortality, but also anchors us to the Infinite, by blessing us with a perception that is eternal. Families that are bound together by covenants made with God provide a much needed longitudinal perspective in those societies where just about everything, including relationships, is increasingly disposable. When there has been no deposit made, there can be no expectation of a return.

Those of God's children
who have grown to His spiritual
stature will employ the Sabbath as a
vehicle to approach His dwelling place,
to behold "the transcendent beauty of the
gate through which the heirs of that kingdom
will enter, which (is) like unto circling flames
of fire; Also the blazing throne of God, wherein
(shall be) seated the Father and the Son." And
the "beautiful streets of that kingdom" will
appear to be paved with gold. (D&C 137:
2-4). This beautiful imagery describes
the power that is inherent in the Law
of the Sabbath, that can make our
lives sublime, as we leave
behind our footprints
on the sand of
time.

Over
a period of
time, we slowly
evolve into revelatory
receptacles of spiritual
energy during our Sabbath
worship services. We witness
an amazing truth: "That which
is of God is light, and he that
receiveth light, and continueth in
God, receiveth more light, and that
light groweth brighter and brighter
until the perfect day."
(D&C 50:24).

As we gather on the Sabbath, we are unified, even as our worship service recognizes our diversity. It quickly moves us away from dependence and independence, to interdependence. However, it blesses us with unity and conformity without asking us to give up our individuality, or those things that make us unique. It invites us to come unto God and to "partake of his goodness; (for) he denieth none that come unto him, black and white, bond and free, male and female; and he remembereth the heathen; and all are alike unto God, both Jew and Gentile." (2 Nephi 26:33).

The principles and doctrines we teach in our Sabbath day school were not just designed that we might live as families forever. They were also created to teach us how to live now, how to appreciate the dominion enjoyed by God, how to use the tools He has given to us, and how to create a heaven on earth where we may retain a hope of eternal life even as we vigorously engage mortality. Carpe diem!

Without
the spiritual and
priesthood power that is
renewed on the Sabbath, we must
remain ever learning, while never
coming to a knowledge of the truth
that would make us free. We grasp at
straws, failing to recognize that nothing
will kill our creativity more quickly than
the self-assurance that poisons our ability
to recognize the influence of powers
that are greater than ourselves.

The activities of
the Sabbath day leave
us heavy with anticipation,
as we eagerly look forward to
the third act of the Three Act Play,
and to the final pages of the script,
where, having prayed ourselves hot,
we will read ourselves full and let
ourselves go, to live happily ever
after in that magical kingdom
where our dreams really do
come true.

The Apostle Paul knew what it meant to give his heart to the Savior. He ministered to the Corinthian Saints, whom he was pleased to learn had a working relationship with the laws and ordinances of the Gospel. He characterized their unassuming faith as being written upon "tables of stone." That is well and good, but he hinted that there exists a second order of mind, or a connection that can be ours if we will embrace our Sabbath day services: "Ye are manifestly declared to be the epistle of Christ ministered by us, written not with ink, but with the Spirit of the living God; not in tables of stone, but in the fleshy tables of the heart."
(2 Corinthians 3:3).

It makes very little difference to our Father whether we are combating the influence of the Seven Deadly Sins, or the garden-variety of transgressions that we commit daily. The Law of the Sabbath stipulates that when we have sinned, we must go thru a process of repentance to be admitted into the presence of the Lord.

All of
us will be
tested by trials
and temptations,
and we will make
mistakes. But we will
rise above our failures
because of our love of the
Savior and His Atonement. It
is in the next act that all the
mysteries will be solved, all the
pieces of the puzzle will be put in
their proper place, all the confusion
that had aforetime tormented us will
be put to rest, and everything will be
made right. For that to occur, we
need to be up and about, starting
right now, by making our way
to our Sabbath day services
in the wards and stakes
of Zion.

Our Sabbath
day services ask us to do
more than sit back and dream
about the rapture. We must organize
ourselves, and "prepare every needful
thing; and establish a house, even a house
of prayer, a house of fasting, a house of faith
a house of learning, a house of glory, (and) a
house of order." (D&C 88:119). In effect, we
must create and maintain a house that has
been dedicated to God, that we might
inherit not only immortality, which
is freely given to all, but also
the greater gift of eternal
life, which is reserved
for the obediently
faithful.

Some
ask: "What
do I want out
of life?" But those
who have unleashed
Sabbath day magic,
instead ask:" What
would my Savior
have me do?"

The
Sabbath day
helps us as we
exercise our capacity
to look beyond telestial
temptations and temporal
trivia. It blesses us with the
will to adjust our perspective
so that the Atonement becomes
a powerful motivator for good
as it removes the stain of sin
from the tapestry that is the
tableau of our lives in the
telestial winter of the
lone and dreary
world.

With
the guidance
that we receive
on the Sabbath day, it
becomes possible for us
to negotiate the strait and
narrow path all the way to
the Tree of Life, there to
partake of its delicious
fruit, which represents
eternal life.

The ways of the world can leave us vulnerable to a spiritual sickness that imitates the symptoms of those who have advanced diabetes. When our peripheral circulation has been compromised, we will become numb to the better angels of our nature and we can lose our capacity to feel the power of Jesus during our Sabbath day worship.

To have the
unlimited freedom
to choose for ourselves
in an atmosphere that is so
full of dangerous deceptions,
enticing entrapments, soothing
seductions, and perilous pathways,
entails great risk. On the Sabbath, we
are introduced to a sanctuary that is
remarkably untainted from the blood
and sins of this generation, where we
may flee from Spiritual Babylon to
faithfully exercise our agency to
be, and more importantly,
to become.

Those
of us who
doggedly make
our way to Sabbath
day worship to enjoy
its quiet serenity, and to
partake of the fruit of the
Tree of Life, must negotiate
a treacherous path past great
and spacious buildings that
dot the landscapes of our
lives, and that invite us
to pause for a while,
to partake of their
pleasures.

We can
never hope to
find meaning in
our empty lives if
we treat the integral
elements of our Sabbath
day services superficially,
if we disregard its ordinances,
or if we treat our covenants with
recklessness. The combined ability
of their power to bless our lives must
be earned. If we take them for granted,
or if our vessels remain devoid of the oil
of gladness because we have abandoned
the core teachings of the holy Sabbath,
our appreciation of their significance
may be slip away just at the critical
moment when the Bridegroom is
about to make His entrance at
the wedding feast.

The
Law of
the Sabbath
has real meaning
only to those who have
accepted God and Christ,
have entered the fold thru
the covenant of baptism, and
have received the Holy Ghost.
These are they who have made
a conscious determination to
serve faithfully and endure
to the end of their days,
in righteousness.

The Law
of the Sabbath was
written to legally secure our
eternal legacy, so that there will
be no gaps in our family histories,
no names missing from the book of
life that has been carefully compiled
by angels taking notes in heaven, and
no empty seats around the table, when
we all sit down together to enjoy a
reunion at family dinner before
the hearth in our home in the
Celestial Kingdom.

In a way, it is fortunate that the veil keeps us insulated from God's reality, and grounds us on the solid and familiar bedrock of past, present, and future. For now, at least, the arrow of time moves in only one forward direction. This handy frame of reference permits us to live in an orderly fashion within a timeline woven in to the tapestry of Sabbath day services.

Within
the embrace
of our worship on
the Sabbath day, conformity
has the capacity to provide us
with significant sustainable support.
Without the consistency that is one of
the greatest blessings of the Gospel, our
lives would become inconsequential. Such is
the condition of those who are confronted
by the sense of futility that accompanies
their failure to focus on the sense of
community that is stimulated by our
obedience to the foundation
principles of the Law
of the Sabbath.

As the Saints busily engage themselves in the organization of Sabbath day worship services, every needful thing must be prepared, to create "a house of learning, even a house of prayer, a house of fasting, a house of faith, a house of learning, a house of glory, a house of order, (and) a house of God" (D&C 88:119).

In our Sabbath worship, there may come a time when we "see the light." We may be dazzled by an A-ha! moment, when we have an instant of sudden insight, intuition, comprehension, inspiration, recognition, or even revelation.

On the
Sabbath day, we
get our bearings
on eternity and we
take a fix on the stars
in the heavens. It is then
that our telestial tendencies
are transformed into celestial
sureties. This process is not one
of maturation, but of generation,
and we are "born again" in a
delivery room that is open
24 x 7, but in particular,
on the Sabbath day.

Knowing that the Sabbath exists, gives us a measure of hope that we will continue to be able to utilize the tools the Lord provides to make the vital distinction between knowledge and wisdom, and to use them to make correct choices that are based upon the intelligent application of the former in order to experience the latter.

On the Sabbath,
in moments of deep
reflection as we soak in
the mysteries, we learn that
we are begotten spirit children of
Heavenly parents, and that we lived
in our pre-mortal existence with them
before we began our sojourn on earth.
We experience moments of déjà vu,
when with awakened memories we
realize that we are pilgrims and
strangers on earth who have
wandered from a more
exalted sphere.

Before we commit to any significant course of action, such as attending Sabbath day worship services with consistency, we make the issue a matter of prayer, so that we may experience the confirming witness of the Spirit. Then, when we have received fire for the deed, we cannot fail.

The Sabbath
day of the Lord
blesses us with courage
to be "witnesses of God at
at all times and in all things,
and in all places." (Mosiah 18:9).
We join with a chorus of voices that
testifies of His might, majesty, power,
and dominion. We dare not shirk our
opportunities, for we are under
covenant to seize the
moment.

Our careful and prayerful study of scripture helps us to obtain an eternal perspective. Jacob revealed the formula. He said "We search the prophets, and we have many revelations and the spirit of prophecy; and having all these witnesses we obtain a hope, and our faith (in Christ is) unshaken." (Jacob 4:6).

The Sabbath day is a great time to learn the grammar of the Gospel. It is the exclamation point of our repentance process. We approach our worship with confidence that "at the banquet of consequences, we will be able to bow our heads in reverence, rather than hang them in shame, in the presence of God who will be there."
(Marion D. Hanks).

Moses counseled the Israelites to build upon the Rock of their salvation. He urged them to "write (their covenants) upon the posts of (their) houses" and not "to appear before the Lord empty" handed. (Deuteronomy 6:9 & 16:16). We would do well to do likewise, by summoning our covenant to remember the Sabbath day and to keep it holy, as we take upon ourselves the name of Christ, and promise to be obedient, and to always remember Him.

May we so live
that we are never more
than a week away from the
last time we have honored the
Sabbath day; so that when it is
time for heaven to reach out and
sweep us up into its embrace, we
will be prepared to respond in
kind, with open arms and
an engaging smile on
our face.

There is no fanfare
on the Sabbath day; just
quiet reflection, meditation,
contemplation, introspection,
and a deep desire to draw near
to our Father. Though our flesh
and our hearts may fail, God
is our strength and our
portion forever.

If we ignore the blessings of the Sabbath day, we are guilty of turning away our faces from the habitation of the Lord. Because the people of Judah disregarded both the temple and its related ordinances, 2 Chronicles 29:8 reveals that the wrath of the Lord was upon them and upon Jerusalem, and He "delivered them to trouble, to astonishment, and to hissing."

We are not, and
never wish to be, lights
unto ourselves. We cannot
overcome the world on our own.
But when, on the Sabbath day, we borrow
the Lord's strength and power, we can do
all things. Many times, He told disobedient
Israel that His "hand is stretched out still."
(Isaiah 10:4). If we ignore it, or if we
refuse His invitation to lift us up, we
invite disaster. Our behavior must
ignite the power of humility,
so that the meek can
inherit the earth.

Our Sabbath day worship takes us through the portal of personal preparedness, accountability, and responsibility, in the direction of celestial sureties that have not only been encompassed by an expanding circle of opportunity, but that have also been embraced by the perfect law of liberty. Our covenants, and in particular the privilege of partaking of the Sacrament, make us feel as if we have been born again, through a spiritual birth canal that delivers us into the Lord's Rest and eternal life.

On the
Sabbath, our souls
are released to go forth
from their dwelling places,
to discard the poor lenses of
our bodies, and peer through
the telescope of truth into
the infinite reaches of
immortality.

With latter-day revelation and instruction on the Sabbath, we still only dimly perceive our noble heritage, and we sometimes find it hard to accept the fact that we mingled among the Gods before our mortal births.

When we determine to honor the Sabbath, we think of the observation of Dag Hammarskjöld: "The longest journey is the journey inward, for those who have chosen their destiny have started upon a quest for the source of their being."

The virtue of the
Sabbath day is its ability to
touch our hearts, to change our
nature, to soften us and to humble
us, to make us as pliant clay in the
hands of the Master Potter, to mold
us as children, and to securely
envelop us in the happiness
that has been prepared
for the Saints.

Heavenly Father has given us the Sabbath that we might aim high. With its perspective, we discard the poor lenses of the body, with its myopic view of life, and look instead up to the rolling vistas of eternity.

The revelatory
reassurance that flows
as a balm of Gilead on
the Sabbath day of the Lord
spectacularly responds to our
needs. With a vision clear and
unobstructed, it sees the clouds
before they have appeared on
our horizons, and it issues
timely weather bulletins
in our behalf.

The Sabbath grounds us, not on telestial turf that is soiled with the stain of sin, but on broad celestial boulevards that have been paved with shining bricks of the appearance of 24 carat gold. Of a truth, our Father in Heaven dwells in the midst of everlasting burnings.

There
are markers
on the chart that is
unfurled on the Sabbath
day of the Lord, upon which
are revealed the boundaries and
the conditions that had aforetime
delineated the unknown possibilities
of existence. We accept the challenge
to expand both our minds and our
horizons, to scribe a circle that
encompasses the solid footing
of the sod of the Sabbath,
as opposed to the shaky
ground of telestial
turf.

The Holy Ghost is our mentor and our teacher. If we are good students, and we have completed all of our homework assignments, participation in Sabbath day worship services will reward us with an illumination of the principles of The Plan of Salvation that will bathe our minds with a revelatory cascade of insight, intuition, and inspiration that streams forth in a downpour of divine direction. It will bless us as we walk along illuminated pathways, and as we exercise our faculties of mind and spirit. The Sabbath leads us to the community of Christ, so that, together, we may enjoy guidance from the Holy Ghost.

As our families are unified by their obedience to the laws that relate to the Sabbath day, they learn about the temporal and the spiritual principles of government that relate to their families.

We persevere in
our observance of the
Sabbath day, "Till we all
come in the unity of the faith
and of the knowledge of the Son
of God ... unto the measure of
the stature of the fulness of
Christ." (Ephesians 4:13).

Our Sabbath observances teach patience, even in the face of challenges when our portion seems unfair, when our difficulties seem unreasonable, and when the proportions of the problems looming before us seem daunting.

Sabbath day worship is just the prescription the Doctor ordered to treat the religious fever that elevates our testimony temperature enough to get our juices flowing with a visceral appreciation of the sacrifice of the Savior thru His Atonement.

What we learn on the Sabbath day helps us to redefine and redesign what had heretofore been stumbling blocks. They are repurposed into the very stepping stones that are needed to fortify our confidence, conquer our fears, and overcome the mental and emotional obstacles all of us will encounter as we move along the yellow brick road on the path of our progression.

Stubborn souls who refuse to obey the Law of the Sabbath look instead to gods of wood and stone that may only temporarily soothe their temporal and spiritual trauma. But, ultimately, it is only the Atonement of Christ that can redeem them from their self-induced misery.

Sabbath
day worship
encourages us
to fix our sights
on the pole-star of
the Atonement, that
was designed to lift
us to higher plateaus
of personal progress.
Work we must, but
our lunch is free,
provided by the
Savior of the
world.

If we
examine it
closely, we will
discover thru our
Sabbath day worship
that within the fabric
of the material that is
our lives' tapestries, are
"dark threads that are as
needful in the Weaver's
skillful hand, as are the
threads of gold and of
silver, in the pattern
He has planned."
(B. Franklin).

The HazMat
Protocols of the
Sabbath day have been
written into The Plan to
detoxify us from the cares
and conditioning influences
of the world, and to neutralize
the homogenization process that
takes place as we are worn down
by the vagaries of men and the
vicissitudes of life.

The
Sabbath day
gives each of us
the opportunity to be
repetitively re-vitalized, as
we are re-introduced to that
magical kingdom where our hopes
and our dreams really do come true,
and we all live happily ever after. When
we wish upon the star of Jesus Christ, it will
make no difference who we are. Anything
our hearts desire will come to us. If we
put our hearts and our souls into our
dreams, no request will be
too extreme.

The Great Plan that
was created by our Father
in Heaven envisions a Utopian
society, but it is also pragmatic.
It anticipated our weaknesses and
provided us with the Sabbath as a
practical solution for those of
us whose agency would lead
us away from the Rod of
Iron, along the strait
and narrow way.

We discover a reservoir of
strength that is sufficient for our
needs in our Sabbath day activities.
As we continue to seek the Lord while
He may be found, a constant companion
will teach us how we may become better
engaged in fashioning defensive weapons
in our armory of thought. It is with these
tools that the Spirit will guide us and
direct us. He will show us just what
we need to do in order to build
our heavenly fortifications of
love, joy, strength, service,
compassion, testimony,
conversion, and
peace.

Honoring the
Sabbath day anchors
us within Gospel topsoil,
that is nourished by an
underground river of living
water. We immerse ourselves
in worship on this holiest of
days. Our devotions are our
expression of honesty with
ourselves, with our Father,
with the Redeemer of the
world, and finally, with
the Holy Ghost.

Our fidelity is focused on the Savior on the Sabbath. It nurtures our relationship with God, and with the Holy Ghost, as well. If we hope to become the architects of our own destiny, we must first identify, and then learn to rely upon, these resources that are, and will forever be, infinitely greater than ourselves. Who could ask for better role-models?

I will go before your face," the Lord has promised. "I will be on your right hand, and on your left, and my Spirit shall be in your hearts, and mine angels round about you, to bear you up." (D&C 84:88). With such assurance, how could we think to turn away from our Sabbath day activities, by persisting in our wicked ways, and by flying solo without a parachute, over the sprawling landscapes of our lives?

Our
Sabbath Day
activities bless
us to employ intrinsic
countermeasures to wicked
imaginations. Our behavior is
driven by altruism, self-denial,
self-discipline, self-restraint,
and self-sacrifice. These all
come as we listen with our
hearts to the promptings
of the Spirit that are as
the quiet whispers of
a gentle breeze.

Those
who decline
the offer of the
riches of eternity that
are unfolded to us during
our Sabbath worship services
are doomed to live their lives
in scarcity of their spiritual
needs. They live beneath
the poverty level, and
may not even be
aware of it.

It is on
the Sabbath day that
our innate longing to be
clean finds expression in the
celestial sparks that are struck
off the divine anvil of God. They
ignite our desire to repent of our
sins. Instruction in Sabbath schools
promises not only eternal life, but
also immortal love. Death becomes
a horizon that is nothing, save the
limit of our sight, and we perish
only when we lose the vision
of our heavenly home.

The Devil has always been a deceiver and a con man, and he was a liar from the beginning, when he tried to foil the execution of The Plan of Salvation and progression of all of God's children, by the substitution of his counterfeit proposal. That desperate and unworkable alternative would have stipulated none of the Sabbath devotions with which we are familiar, and that vitalize our faith. Fortunately, at the Council in Heaven, when both plans were discussed, we were able to see through his deception. Here on earth, we have retained our eternal perspective, and our behavior reflects our continuing determination to exercise our agency to remain as disciples of Christ.

Those who can really appreciate the power of the Sabbath day of the Lord are able to visualize the Celestial Kingdom. They use the Atonement of Christ to move in its direction. They follow the admonition of the Savior: "Seek ye first the kingdom of God, and his righteousness; and all these things shall be added unto you." (Matthew 6:33).

Solemn promises that
are expressed during our
Sabbath day services initiate an
introspective cleansing of our souls.
The process of our sanctification thru
the Atonement allows us to draw near
to God's throne in heaven. As we do
so, we acknowledge His omniscient
power, and that He will bestow
upon us blessings we need,
instead of those that we
only thought we
wanted.

Our
abiding faith
in the divine Plan
of our Father in Heaven
is confirmed on the Sabbath,
where we learn that it has been
designed to bring us back into His
kingdom after we have grown up unto
the Lord, have spiritually matured,
and have demonstrated that the
basis of our hope of salvation
is in His Atonement, and
that alone.

An understanding
of our pre-mortal existence,
as it unfolds at our Sabbath day
instruction in the stakes of Zion,
sanctifies life, dignifies individual
effort, and rewards achievement.
Most importantly, it recognizes the
Atonement as the pivotal event
of the perfect Plan of
Salvation.

Hell is a reformatory
that has been designed to improve
the quality of our moral nature. It is
a penitentiary where faith can still convict us
of our sins. It was designed to help disobedient
spirits acknowledge the power of the Atonement.
In D&C 76, we learn that the Gospel was taught to
those that prison. If, while there, they accept not
only Christ, but also the fulness of His Gospel,
is it possible that they might one day inherit
celestial glory with the Saints. Surely, this
is why, in our services on the Sabbath
day, we learn about temples, where
vicarious work is performed, not
for just a select few, but for
for all of our kindred
dead.

It is only
our profound obedience
and recurring repentance that
release us from the bondage of
sin, and qualify us by worthiness to
enjoy the blessings of the Sabbath. The
Atonement of Jesus Christ, which is the
centerpiece of the instruction that we
receive on the Lord's day, allows us
to overcome our limitations while
unleashing the powers of heaven
in our behalf. It shatters the
bands of death, and pushes
the boundaries of the
Celestial Kingdom
itself.

The Sabbath is the locomotive that helps us to enjoy our ride. We board a train that is bound for glory with a first-class ticket, so that the dust, delays, sidetracks, smoke, cinders and jolts will be a lot more comfortable. The conductor of that train is Jesus Christ, Who provides significant relief from the pressures of the journey by punching our tickets with His Atonement.

We
cannot expect
to comprehend the
language of the Spirit
until we have paid the price,
and for it t happen, we need
to obey the Law of the Sabbath.
We may dismiss its whisperings as
nothing more than the breeze that
causes a gentle rustle of the leaves
in the forest that is our conscience.
It may sound pleasant to our ears,
but its quiet counsel will remain
maddeningly elusive until we
have done all that we can to
merit the companionship
of the gift of the Holy
Ghost through the
Atonement of
Christ.

Telestial
E.M.T.s are at a
total loss for diagnosis,
while the supernal gift of the
Sabbath day provides a virtual war
chest of therapies for cold, stony,
and hard hearts. Our faith in the
merits of Jesus Christ is the
remedy of choice for
reconciliation.

New converts and well-established members alike find their way to the temple, where they echo Paul, who declared to the Church: "We, being many, are one body in Christ." (Romans 12:5). The spiritual unification of the Saints has been repetitively confirmed in the universally recognizable ripple effects that range from simple Sabbath day services to more formal worship services in the House of the Lord.

As we make our way to our Sabbath day services, it will be as it was in the days of King Josiah, when he "went up into the house of the Lord, and all the men of Judah and all the inhabitants of Jerusalem with him, and the priests, and the prophets, and all the people, both small and great. And (they) made a covenant before the Lord, to walk after the Lord, and to keep his commandments and his testimonies and his statutes with all their heart and all their soul, (and) to perform the words of the covenant. And all the people stood to the covenant." (2 Kings 23:2-3).

As we live in obedience to the covenant we renew on the Sabbath day, we prepare ourselves through sanctification by the Spirit to be led unerringly by the Lord. We take Him at His word, when He says: "Mine angels shall go up before you, and also my presence." (D&C 103:20). Come follow me takes on a whole new meaning.

Faithful participants
in life's Three Act Play are
now and forever independent in
that stage of development to which
their decisions have led them. Poised
at the edge of forever, they need little
incentive other than the activities of
the Sabbath day to push off into
the unknown possibilities
of existence.

Whenever
Latter-day Saints
cannot find resources
within the Church to sustain
their connection to Deity that
had been established on the Sabbath,
they are at risk of sliding back into
marginalized relationships that may even
brand them as "less active," or "inactive."
Fundamentally, they lose direction, power,
and purpose, because they have mislaid the
means to nourish, support, and sustain
interpersonal connections that can
only be powered by principles
that had, in the past, been
their guiding lights.

Heavenly Father has always commanded His people to honor the Sabbath because, in a very real sense, each of us is confined to a world our own making, and most of us are trapped within the narrowly defined perceptual prisons that we create for ourselves. Its walls are reinforced by the razor-wire of limiting beliefs, those stories we tell ourselves that sabotage our own best efforts. Without the endowment of power in the priesthood, they can damage or even cripple our lives by diminishing our abilities, compromising our progress, and preventing us from reaching our worthy goals.

As we attend our
Sabbath schools, we learn
about the best of power and
the worst of violence, and we see
that they are mutually exclusive; where
one is present the other must be absent. We
learn about the satanic inclination to abuse
authority, and we discover that those who have
it may be least prepared for positions of trust
and responsibility. As the drama unfolds, we
discern a simple mathematical theorem:
that the principles of God's perfect
Plan operate more by addition
than by subtraction.

It was Brigham Young's belief that "all organized existence is in progress either to an endless advancement in eternal perfections, or back to dissolution. There is no period in the eternities," he felt, "wherein organized existence will become stationary, that it cannot advance in knowledge, wisdom, glory, and power." (J.D. 1:349). Such are the mind expanding possibilities that we learn about during Sabbath day worship services.

It is through the phenomenon of the continuing, enduring, immeasurable, infinite, uncorrupted, unfathomable, uninterrupted, and unspoiled grace that is embodied within the activities in which we find ourselves engaged on the holy Sabbath that we are "swallowed up in the joy of ... God, even to the exhausting of (our) strength." (Alma 27:17).

The Plan of Salvation
is so magnificent that when
it was presented to those who had
assembled in the Council, "the morning
stars sang together, and all the sons of God
shouted for joy." (Job 38:7-8). The principle of
equality that is taught on the Sabbath makes it
unlikely that a Plan of transcendent perfection
would have been intentionally designed to save
only a small percentage of those children of
promise, in His Celestial Kingdom. To believe
such effectively must dismisses as a thing
of naught His mission statement, which is
to bring to pass their immortality and
eternal life. Instead, we envision no
empty chairs at the table in heaven,
when we sit down with our Father
at the celebration that is our
missionary homecoming. It
may be in the Atonement
that all the sons and
daughters of God
will return with
honor.

As
the kingdom
rapidly grows, the
Lord helps us to bloom
where we are planted. Even
as we recognize and appreciate
our unique qualities, talents, and
experiences, the Sabbath helps us
to be bound together in ways
that bridge cultural chasms
that might otherwise
separate us.

On the Sabbath
day, we learn that
God promises us not
just nurturing rain, but
also the mud that inevitably
follows. It is our lot in life to
dutifully trudge past potholes
and other obstacles on rocky
roads that are uphill most
of the way and that face
into an unrelenting
headwind.

In a sharp contrast to the hectic demands that are put upon us by the world, the Sabbath day generates repetitive opportunities for us to stop and smell the roses along the way during our journey Home. In fact, our Heavenly Father created the roses in the first place, as love letters to His children. Of these subtle reinforcements, the poet wrote: "Earth is crammed with heaven, and every bush with fire of God. But only those who see, take off their shoes. The rest stand around picking blackberries."

When,
on the holy
Sabbath, we turn our
backs on the habitation
of the Lord, we are painting
ourselves into conceptual corners,
limiting our creative expression to a
narrow and confusing rational reality
of our own construction. When we turn
away from the light of our lives, we
may think we have it all, when all
that is before us is an illusion
that is only a shadow and a
caricature of reality.

Latter-day Saints who embrace the Law of the Sabbath have taken their commitment to a new level. They redefine dedication, and they exercise their duties in ways that are truly selfless. The Gospel has transformed their lives. They are as the people of Zarahemla, who declared to King Benjamin: "The Spirit of the Lord Omnipotent ... has wrought a mighty change in us, or in our hearts, that we have no more disposition to do evil, but (instead) to do good continually." (Mosiah 5:2).

As we respond
to the invitations
of the Spirit on the
Sabbath day, there is
something that whispers
to us, telling us that our
trials were not designed to
test our ability, but rather
our availability.

The raw energy of Sabbath day worship helps us to better appreciate God. We feel the divine potential as it swells within our hearts. We confidently ask seemingly simple questions that have profound answers and implications that shake our world. They spread like the ripples that radiate outward from a rock thrown into the still waters of a pond. We begin to see the Sabbath day as a revelatory machine for the making of Gods.

The line in all of
our favorite fairy tales,
that reads: "...and they all
lived happily ever after," was not
written for the second act of life's
Three Act Play, but for the third act.
Nevertheless, on the Sabbath, each time
we participate in our worship services,
we get a foretaste of the happiness
that has been prepared for the
Saints, and that awaits us
just beyond the veil.

The
Sabbath day
detoxifies us
from the cares
of the world and
homogenization of
our standards, even
as we are subjected to
the vicissitudes of life.
It allows us to return to
the hallowed halls of our
meeting house sanctuaries,
to be re-vitalized, as we are
are re-introduced to God's
Magical Kingdom where
dreams really do
come true.

The expanding
circles of opportunity
that are woven into our
Sabbath day services leave no
room for limiting beliefs. It is
within the hallowed walls of the
sanctuary of God that we trade
the indecisive support embraced
by those who have been trapped
in mediocrity, for the certain
guidance that we, along with
our celestial-bound fellow
travelers, will surely
enjoy as a gift of
the Spirit.

The meager substitutes for the rewards of the Sabbath include wealth, affluence, authority, style, influence, position, fashion, and dominion. When lumped together, these become the holy grail of those who engage in a blind quest for the power and control that are the antithesis of the sound doctrine that is illustrated by Sabbath day worship that leads to a cascade of revelatory guidance.

Our Heavenly
Father glories in
the possibility that we
might one day be like Him,
and offers us a special gift on
the Sabbath; pointedly, His grace,
consisting of the gifts and power
by which we may be brought to
His perfection and stature, so
that we may enjoy not only
what He has, but also
what He is.

Our
focus of
attention on the
Savior on the Sabbath
can energize the power of
the Atonement to break the
bands of death, and free us
to enjoy God's grace. "There
is no other name given whereby
salvation cometh," said Benjamin;
"therefore, I would that ye should
take upon you the name of Christ,
all you that have entered into
the covenant with God."
(Mosiah 5:8).

In the
life of every
individual whose
thoughts, words, and
deeds are not in harmony
with the Law of the Sabbath,
there will come a time when
a readjustment must obliterate
the mask of hypocrisy. As painful
as the process of reformation may
be, it is necessary to allow for the
cultivation of the more nurturing
lifestyle that is made possible
only when we embrace the
promises we have made
to keep the Sabbath
day holy.

The priesthood is energized by the grace of God, as it administers the ordinances of salvation, sanctification, justification, and exaltation. These allow us to receive the blessings of the Gospel by binding us to Him through covenants of action. The Law of the Sabbath, in particular, helps us to enjoy a wider perspective of our place in the cosmos, as well as a greater understanding of The Plan of Salvation, and of eternity itself.

The Law
of the Sabbath is
where we must turn
for spiritual security,
and obedience is the only
requirement we must satisfy to
capture its blessings. If we seek
"all the days of (our) lives for that
which (we) cannot obtain, and ... have
sought for happiness in doing iniquity,
which thing is contrary to the nature of
that righteousness which is in our great
and Eternal Head," we must face the
consequences. (Helaman 13:38). It
is then, under the most difficult
circumstances imaginable, that
the uttermost farthing must be
paid to satisfy the demands
of Justice, so the required
reform might finally
take place, that
Mercy might
claim its
own.

Our eyes
become single
to the glory of God
when we catch the vision
of Sabbath day worship. We are
converted to its power, and our
whole bodies are filled with light.
There is no darkness in us, and we
begin to see more clearly. We are
filled with an unearthly light. We
begin to see by the dancing light
of the Holy Ghost. Then, after
our faith has been ignited,
we develop the capacity
to comprehend all
things.

When we have foolishly
built upon the shifting sands of
secular humanism, if we do not have
the Sabbath to which we can turn, where
will our sanctuary be when the winds blow
and the rains beat down upon us? To what safe
harbor will we flee, when the ocean of life is in
turmoil? When we are tossed about as flotsam
and jetsam, never coming to a knowledge of
the truth, to what source will we look for
the stability we so desperately seek, or
for the answers to life's questions
that continually vex our spirits?

After the Flood, the
ancients built ziggurats
that were simply towers that
had been specifically designed
to reach all the way into heaven.
The Tower of Babel is an example of
these exaggerated temple spires. However,
their designers and builders, and those who
flocked to behold these architectural marvels,
missed the point. Instead of creating physical
structures composed of nothing more than
brick and mortar, they could have more
profitably spent their time by using the
principles taught on the Sabbath day
to build enduring relationships
with each other and with
our Heavenly Father.

Even as we honor
our Heavenly Father on
the Sabbath day, our feeble
attempts to describe His majesty
utilize abstractions, for thoughts
cannot be shaped, nor words formed,
nor sentences constructed, that could
possibly accurately articulate His glory.
Figures of speech are employed because
we would otherwise be at a complete loss
for words when grasping for even a basic
explanation of profound metaphysical
realities. To Moses, "the presence of
the Lord appeared (as) a flame of
fire out of the midst of a bush.
And he looked, and, behold,
the bush burned with fire,
and the bush was not
consumed." (J.S.T.
Exodus 3:2).

If we refuse to honor our Heavenly Father on the Sabbath day, it is because we have submitted to blind guides. We have denied not only His power to transform our lives, but also His very grace. We turn our backs on the habitation of the Lord, and We dismiss the sacrifice of His Son. We esteem as a thing of naught His suffering, and we close our minds to soul-expanding opportunities. We are snared by Satan and are bound by his strong chains, and all the while, we thought it was the comfortable feeling of a flaxen cord that had been placed around our necks.

It
is on the
Sabbath that we
get our bearings
on eternity and we
take a fix on the stars
in the heavens. It is then
that our telestial tendencies
are transformed into celestial
sureties. This process is not one
of maturation, but of generation,
as we are "born again" in the
delivery rooms we call the
chapels of the wards and
stakes of Zion.

It is only natural that when we pay our oblations to God on the Sabbath day, it would be on the condition of our worthiness, for the anticipated blessings can only flow when the conduct of our lives harmonizes with the nature of God. On the Sabbath day, we would do well to heed the voice of the Lord, Who commanded Moses from the burning bush on Sinai: "Put off thy shoes from off thy feet, for the place whereon thou standest is holy ground." (Exodus 3:5).

It is in our
Sabbath day worship
services that the Spirit opens
the eyes of our understanding to
undreamed of vistas of otherwise
inaccessible experience. It is there
that we begin to comprehend the
scope of Moroni's promise that
it is "by the power of the Holy
Ghost that (we) may know
the truth of all things."
(Moroni 10:5).

The light and
knowledge that we
receive in Sabbath day
school set us free from
the limitations of our own
ignorance, as well as from the
wobbly constraints of mortality.
It is on the Sabbath that we learn to
be at one with a majestic clockwork,
"like a bird that, pausing in her flight
a while on boughs too light, feels them
give way beneath her and yet sings,
knowing that she hath wings."
(Victor Hugo).

It is in Sabbath school
that the depth and breadth of
our comprehension finally puts to
rest the debates that have preoccupied
man since the beginning of the Age of
Reason. We soar to new heights as the
reconciliation between science and
religion harmonizes and clarifies
our understanding of our place
both in the temporal universe
and in the eternities.

"Where there is no vision, the people perish." (Proverbs 29:18). The Sabbath endows us with a view that provides a much more accurate matrix within which we may develop a construct of the universe in which we live. In this sense, the glory of God is our ability to be positively influenced by both the physical and spiritual worlds around us, even the multi-dimensional world that we cannot see with our eyes. The light and truth of intelligence provides a precise representation of the cosmos that affords us the opportunity to clarify our vision to better perceive reality; to see as God does.

Jeremiah knew what it feels like
to internalize the Law of the Sabbath.
He wrote: "His word was in mine heart as
a burning fire shut up in my bones, and I
was weary with forbearing, and I could not
stay." (Jeremiah 2:9). When we do likewise,
our countenances will reflect an unearthly
light, as we are transformed from within.
The world seeks change from the outside,
and fails miserably. The Gospel, on the
other hand, changes us from the inside,
and succeeds brilliantly. We are thus
created to reach our potential in
both the image and likeness
of God our Father.

Even as we
make valiant efforts
to focus the powers of our
intellect on eternal elements,
because we are bounded on all
sides by a crushing present reality,
if our hearts have not been softened
to relate to the things of the Spirit, we
cannot understand the creations of God
except in the most academic, abstract, and
obtuse ways. Joseph Smith explained that we
"must have a change of heart if we wish to
see the kingdom of God." Our Sabbath day
service is a schoolmaster that mentors
us, that our hearts might be softened
to comprehend the things
of God.

Our positive experiences on the Sabbath day that lead us to make good choices are essential to our eternal progression. How we respond now to the invitation to visit the holy habitation of the Lord will determine what blessings and opportunities will be available later.

Our efforts to define heaven and earth by subtraction, rather than by addition, are destined to fail. God's reality is infinitely richer and is far more satisfying than any poor substitute a rational approach might grudgingly concede could exist. The revelation we receive on the Lord's holy day is more than we could ever know by relying only upon the poor lenses of the body, that often reveal a myopic view of life, and are blinded to spirituality.

When we are
at one with God,
when we have spiritually
been born of Him and have
internalized His divine nature,
we will receive His image in our
countenances. That image and His
"likeness" will bridge the barriers of
time and space to leave an indelible
marker as a reminder of our noble
birthright. On the Sabbath day, the
Lord rewrites the genetic code
within each of us to permeate
our spirits with superpowers
that push the boundaries
of heaven and
earth.

"My thoughts are not your thoughts," said the Lord, "neither are your ways my ways ... For as the heavens are higher than the earth, so are my ways higher than your ways, and my thoughts than your thoughts." (Isaiah 55:8-9). His thoughts are loftier, broader, more visionary, and infinitely more expansive. His ways circumscribe the sum of our reality and encompass more than we have ever dared to dream, which is why He has given us the Law of the Sabbath, and has asked us to dedicate that day to Him, that we might partake of His divine nature.

When the
Apostles were
gathered together
with members of the
Church on the Day of
Pentecost, they were all
of one accord in one place.
It was on the first day of
the week, after the Sabbath.
In any event, the scriptures record
that the visitation of the Holy Ghost
from the immortal world ushered in "a
sound from heaven as of a rushing mighty
wind, and it filled all the house where they
were sitting." So dramatic was His appearance,
that "there appeared unto them cloven tongues
like as of fire, and it sat upon each of them."
Its manifestation was so dramatic that "they
were all filled ... and began to speak with
other tongues as the Spirit gave them
utterance." (Acts 2:1-3).

Our greater
understanding of
the Plan of Salvation
that is revealed on the
Sabbath day surely blesses
our lives in many ways. Its
power creates the opportunity
for dynamic change, as wisdom
flows along established channels.
Moreover, personal accountability,
responsibility, and commitment to
obedience expand. A humble need
to serve strengthens the bonds of
brotherhood and sisterhood, and
generates interdependency in a
community of true believers in
which any cultural boundaries
are effectively expunged. We
are no more strangers or
foreigners, but become
fellowcitizens with
the Saints in the
household of
God.

We
think of
of our Sabbath
day journey, and
recall the wisdom of
Winston Churchill, who
said: "There comes for each
of us that special moment when
we are figuratively tapped on the
shoulder and offered a chance to do
a very special thing, unique to ourselves
and fitted to our talents. What a tragedy
if that moment should find us unprepared or
unqualified for that which might have been our
finest hour." On that day, when we stand before
God, angels, and witnesses at the veil that
separates mortality from eternity, our
report will summarize our finest
hours that were spent in our
worship services on the
Sabbath day.

If we have not worked hard to acquire the perspective of the Sabbath day, we are much more likely to define ourselves only in the present tense. Then, we will be less inclined to make the kinds of decisions that reflect our noble lineage, or to independently develop the attitudes and habit patterns that will bring us, once again, into conformity with heaven. Our ability to "be" may be secure, but our ability to "become" will never be nurtured. Without the Sabbath, we are destined to wither on the vine.

Joseph Smith may have been referring to the instruction that we receive on the Sabbath day, when he wrote: "This is good doctrine. It tastes good. I can taste the principles of eternal life, and so can you. They are given to me by the revelations of Jesus Christ; and I know that ... you believe them. I can taste the spirit of eternal life. I know it is good, and when I tell you of these things which were given me by inspiration of the Holy Spirit, you are bound to receive them as sweet, and rejoice."

Who is it that shall
enjoy the rest of God?
"He that walketh righteously,
and speaketh uprightly; he that
despiseth the gain of oppressions,
that shaketh his hands from holding
of bribes, that stoppeth his ears from
hearing of blood, and shutteth his eyes
from seeing evil. He shall dwell on high.
(His eyes) shall behold the land that is
very far off." (Isaiah 34:14-17). We
prepare ourselves for that journey
of faith, beginning right now, by
honoring the Sabbath day.

Sooner or later,
when we have attended
our worship services on the
Sabbath frequently enough that
our lives have begun to conform to
the character of God, we will enjoy the
realm of spirit as our natural environment
and we will see that it is more vibrantly real
than anything we have ever known. In the
meantime, we beware, lest we strangle
ourselves by illusions of reality, and
with things whose opacity obstructs
our ability to see what is
really there.

To those who have
lived sheltered lives, and
who are unfamiliar with travel
through harsh environments, palms
often seem to grow in desert wastes.
It is only upon closer inspection that
oases of underlying currents of water
may be noticed, that bring nourishment
to the roots of the thirsty trees. So, too,
our worship service on the Sabbath day
is as a storehouse of bread. It is as
a reservoir of living water, whose
flowing fountains of revelation
provide sustenance to all who
hunger and thirst after
righteousness, in the
arid climate of
Idumea.

Those who observe the Law of the Sabbath will learn how to harness their priesthood power to command the elements, to divide and dry up waters, and to turn them out of their course; to put at defiance the armies of nations, to divide the earth and break every band, to stand in the presence of God, and to do all things according to His will and command. They will learn how to subdue principalities and powers with the confident expectation of one day being translated, to be taken up into heaven, as in a whirlwind. (J.S.T. Genesis 14:30-32).

It is on
the Sabbath,
that we are able
to see beyond our
mortal horizons. We
even have a name for
such a state, calling it
"the depths of eternity."
Our covenants bless us to
"inherit thrones, kingdoms,
principalities, powers, (and)
dominions, (of) all heights
and depths." (D&C 132:19).
This begs the question: In
what direction will these
"heights and depths"
lead us?

Brigham Young declared: "How many kingdoms of glory there are, I know not; and how many degrees of glory there are in these kingdoms, I know not; but there are multitudes of them. The kingdoms that God has prepared are innumerable." (J.D., 8:154). Perhaps our discussion of principles and doctrines of the kingdom, on the Sabbath, is but a prelude to our awakening comprehension of the glory and wonder of eternal worlds without number.

The Sabbath
prepares us for
the realization that
our mortal experience
is a tiny fraction of a much
larger reality, and that as long
as we believe our perspective to be
unique, it is faulty. The veil helps us to
appreciate the truth that mortality is not
our natural dimension. We discover why we
could never be entirely comfortable in our
circumstances, and why we sometimes felt
like strangers and pilgrims on the earth.
The experiences we have as we obey the
Law of the Sabbath explain our innate
upward thrust always toward the
future, always beyond the
limited horizon of our
telestial sight.

After we have attended our Sabbath day worship services a few thousand times, we realize that growing old is simply a feature of mortality that was designed by God as a brilliant mechanism that would afford us the opportunity to measure the approach of our engagement with Him in the eternal world, in a reunification that will outlast time and endure throughout all eternity.

Obedience to the Law of the Lord on 52 Sabbath days every year helps us to fathom that when we kill time, we damage our eternal selves, for as the Lord warned, "in an hour when ye think not the summer shall be past, and the harvest ended, and your souls not saved." (D&C 45:2). We realize that with the passage of every second of every day, we are one tick of the clock closer to an "undiscovered country from whose bourne no traveler returns." (Shakespeare).

It is not
the point of
the Sabbath day
to give us a second
wind in the first mile
of the race, when we have
only just begun our journey.
When we are caught up in the
trauma of temporal traps, because
we have allowed our faith to become
so flawed that we have been blinded to
the impotence of our false gods, sooner
or later, the misery that we have created
will catch up to us. Without the bursts of
energy that flow from observing the Law
of the Sabbath on a continuing basis, we
must feel confused, abandoned, and
disillusioned because of our focus
on the fleeting pleasures of the
world, and we will perish
in Babylon.

Our reverence for the
Sabbath day sensitizes us to
spirituality and prepares us to
take action. The veil separating us
from our destiny becomes practically
transparent. We sense the expansion of
God's powers, as the glittering facets
of the life of the Spirit wash over us.
Quiet spiritual stirrings grow into
a force with the power to propel
us into the presence of beings
from the unseen world.
Such is the potential
of the Law of the
Sabbath.

Many
pursue happiness
with a passion, and yet
they are unable to grasp
it. They don't realize that
their failure is tied to the Law
of the Sabbath. Happiness is really
like a butterfly. If we chase it, we
will never catch it. But if we quietly
contemplate the beauty and symmetry
of the Sabbath day, and if we actively
obey the Law of the Lord, His joy and
a peace that surpasses understanding
will come and rest gently on our
shoulders. Perhaps that is what
is meant by the rest of
the Lord.

We
cannot
hope to find
meaning in our
lives if we treat the
elements of the Sabbath
superficially or carelessly.
A conscious appreciation of
their value must be earned. If
we take them for granted, or if
we abandon the principles that are
taught in the classrooms of Zion,
their power to bless our lives
will slip away and be lost.

If we do not
allow our Sabbath day
worship to bless us with the
strength to endure the hard
lessons that life throws our way
with frustrating frequency, we will
look elsewhere for the gods of wood
and stone that may temporarily soothe
our temporal trauma. But deep down
inside, we know that these quick
fixes will never permanently
redeem us from our
misery.

The Sabbath day invites us to become engaged and energized as we journey through Idumea at an unhurried and yet productive pace. It captivates us by its complexity. We are immersed in its intricacies, riveted by its rewards, and wrapped up in its wonders. It patiently anticipates our acknowledgement of its power to transform our lives and guide us to the gates of heaven. It only waits upon our initiative.

Worship
on the Sabbath
catalyzes a state of
innocence and holiness.
The dazzling light of truth
makes manifest the nature of
evil that is abroad in the land,
but our faith gives us power
to prevail over that spirit
of darkness.

Those of weak
character think that
they can circumvent the
performance requirements
of the Sabbath day, but this is
because they have never enjoyed
the experiences of those whose home
turf is the strait and narrow path.
They confuse wicked behavior
with happiness, mistaking
nature for nobility.

Young people talk about "Best Friends Forever," but Heavenly Father would rather have us "Be Forever Faithful" through bonds of obedience to the principles, doctrines, ordinances, and covenants that are taught on the Sabbath day.

If we turn our backs
on the habitation of the Lord
on the Sabbath day, we decline His
offer to experience life abundantly.
We ignore His invitation to come follow
Him. We are deaf to His entreaty to search
out righteousness, and to find in Him
every good thing. Living for the
moment, we die as to the
things of the Spirit.

The Sabbath provides for our religious recalibration thru repentance. It allows us to become reinvigorated by a refreshing celestial breeze. The Law of the Lord paints a portrait of free-will that allows us to take risks. If we fail to abide by the principles of the Gospel, the Savior will always be there to step in and intervene in our behalf, by using the bargaining chip of the Atonement to satisfy the demands of Justice, and claim Mercy on our behalf.

On the
Sabbath, we go to
a place where we are
able to shelter our spirits
and quiet our racing hearts.
We grasp the horns of sanctuary,
so that we might relieve the tensions
that always threaten to overwhelm us,
were we to allow ourselves to be caught
up and remain in the fast lane of life.
The sanctuary of the Sabbath is a time
and a place where we can quietly
reflect on the quality of our
preparation to live with
our Heavenly Father
for eternity.

When those who do not feel worthy to join the Saints in their Sabbath services are able to make behavioral changes, and if they can then modify their nature so that as they mature, their character more fully reflects that of their Father, perhaps they will then feel comfortable at His hearth and home, on earth and in heaven. Surely, the story of the Prodigal Son, that is set against the backdrop of the Atonement of Jesus Christ, lends its support to this thesis.

Those
who grapple with
the permutations and
combinations that we face
in Sabbath day worship services
realize that the key of knowledge
may be employed by both those who
are in poverty and those who abound
in wealth. It is engaged by both fame
and obscurity, exercised in sickness and
in health, put to good use by those with
influence as well as by those who are
living in anonymity, and it may be
successfully retained by both
the beauty and the beast.

Sabbath
day worshipers
enjoy a harmony
in spite of different
cultural, social, political,
or economic circumstances.
All over the world, ordinances
that characterize the Sabbath day
are understood without discussion
or ambiguity. They are administered
by a vast priesthood army whose
striking similarities overshadow
any perceived differences.

On the
Sabbath day, as
our testimony of
Christ swells in our
hearts, faith intensifies
our desire to repent. Our
effort to maintain temple
worthiness centers our lives
to bring us into harmony with
true principles. As we endeavor
to be obedient, we find ourselves
in a constant state of improvement.
We begin to believe in ourselves,
and in God. Our hearts race
with the realization that our
progress might be headed
in the direction of
perfection, after
all.

The activities
of the Sabbath day
set us free to be creative,
and our creativity sets us free to
properly plan before we come face to
face with the crises of life. Our instruction
prevents our poor performance or mitigates
its consequences. We learn to rely upon the
doctrine of Christ as it is taught in worship
services, and internalize its elements. This
permits us to surrender ourselves to its
infinite possibilities. Therein, we find
our individuality, avenues for our
personal expression, and in
the end, we discover our
freedom to "become,"
within the embrace
of God's divine
design.

We embrace our
Sabbath day worship services,
because it is there that we receive
needed transfusions of a spiritual
element. They are heavenly dialysis
centers, where worldly contaminants
may be removed from our systems,
because we are simply incapable
of accomplishing the task on
our own. The resources we
need are only found in
the Atonement of
Christ.

In our Sabbath day worship, our mystical relationship with God becomes indelibly etched within our spiritual identity. We are perfected in our faith to make a link with Deity. That is how members of The Church of Jesus Christ of Latter-day Saints have the presumption to declare that it is our destiny to rule as kings and queens, priests and priestesses, in the house of Israel forever, to reign with authority over kingdoms, thrones, principalities, powers, dominions, and exaltations. That will happen only when our connection to God has reached such a magnitude and strength that our identities become indistinguishable from each other. That can only occur when we have received both His image and His likeness in our countenances in the process of a mind-bending spiritual metamorphosis that defies any rational explanation, and incomprehensively expands the boundaries of our faith.

The originality
and resourcefulness
of the mind of God are such
that He designed Sabbath worship
with redundant mechanisms that would
provide us with repetitive opportunities to
pause for analysis, reflection, commitment,
and renewal, while miraculously minimizing
our tendency to focus inward. As our lives
conform to its principles, we find our
greatest expression, and self-doubt
or second-guessing is virtually
eliminated.

We try
to faithfully
attend our Sabbath
day services, because
we have testimonies of
the divinity of the work.
We are liberated from fear,
doubt, the apprehension of
danger, religious turmoil,
and from the vagaries
of conspiring men
and women as
we do so.

Our places of
Sabbath day devotions
are as revelatory observatories
within which we look up at the stars,
to see heaven before our eyes, through the
clarifying lens of eternity. The incorruptible
aether on the Sabbath day infuses us with the
Spirit, that we may distinguish between right
and wrong, light and darkness, and good
and evil; in short, to make choices that
are founded on celestial certainties,
without the telestial distortion of
atmospheric pollution.

Our
covenants
that are tied to
the Sabbath day help
in myriad ways to unify
the Saints, who are a lot like
snowflakes. Although delicate in
structure, look at what they can do
when they stick together! The Church
and kingdom has need of every member,
that the whole may be kept in perfect
working order, so that all those who
wish to worship may be free to
expand their capabilities and
stretch their potential, in
a forum of free will
and faith.

When we are
steadfast in our
observance of the
Sabbath day, we will
enjoy a knowledge of
the truth, and will be of
a sound understanding. We
search the scriptures diligently,
that we might recognize the word
of God, and because we fast and
pray, we have the spirit of prophecy,
and of revelation, and when we
teach, we do so with the power
and authority of God.
(Sew Alma 17:2-3).

Our attendance at Sabbath services only wanes because it is easy to be distracted by the desire to obtain what we do not need, and to amass what we do not deserve; to hoard what we have not earned, and to stockpile what we cannot ultimately control. Each fall and winter, millions of unvaccinated people succumb to the effects of an influenza that rears its ugly head itself in frustratingly mutated forms, but more die spiritually because they are infected by avarice, greed, covetousness, lust, and pride. Rather than seeking the Lord and establishing His righteousness, they walk in their own way, and after the manner of their own gods.

Profound obedience
and recurring repentance
release us from the bondage of
sin, and qualify us by worthiness to
enjoy the blessings of the Sabbath. The
Atonement of Jesus Christ, which is the
centerpiece of the instruction that is
the focus of our worship, permits us
to overcome our limitations while
unleashing the powers of heaven
in our behalf. It shatters the
glass ceiling of death, and
throws open the gates of
the Celestial Kingdom
itself.

If we
want to be
strictly obedient to
the Sabbath, we cannot
maintain a vacation home
in Idumea as our intermittent
refuge from life on the strait and
narrow path. Such diversions will cause
us to lose traction, impede our forward
momentum, derail us from our footing
on Gospel sod, and delay our progress
toward our determined destination
that has been envisioned by the
foreknowledge of God.

Some think
that they can
be happy if they
wander and play.
They don't consider
that a key feature of
the Sabbath day is that it
encourages us to ponder
and pray, and to study and
apply doctrine and principles.
If we disregard the elements of
the Law of the Sabbath, our old
habit patterns will leave us
more vulnerable to the
enticements of the
adversary.

The deceiver,
who is the enemy of all
good things, finally betrays his
followers. They can only oppose the Law
of the Sabbath for so long before his cunning
caresses lead them into conceptual cul-de-sacs,
religious roundabouts, and doctrinal dead-ends
from which all possible exits lead to confusion,
uncertainty, doubt, ambiguity, hesitancy, and a
retreat that plunges them headlong into a
perceived freedom that is, on closer
inspection, a bottomless pit
of misery.

Heavenly Father
wants us to burst beyond
our self-imposed limitations.
That is why He has ordained a Sabbath,
so that we may one day attain His stature
and become all that He now is. But we may
do this only if we incorporate into our
own being and nature His image and
likeness. Thru that process, He has
ordained that our corruptible
bodies will become clean,
pure, and pulsing
with light.

The Law of the Sabbath requires uncorrupted holiness, that we may more easily feel the sweet influence of the Spirit. Without it, "then wisdom cannot reveal itself, culture cannot become manifest, strength cannot fight, wealth becomes useless, and intelligence cannot be applied." (Heraclitus).

The Law of the Sabbath
provides an unambiguous definition of
eternal truth. It allows us to absorb wisdom
from the events within which we are immersed,
to learn from our relationships with others, to
grow within our environment no matter how
unique or difficult it might seem to us, and
to protect us from the worldly influences
that encroach upon the fortress of our
spiritual security, sanctuary, surety,
and symmetry.

The Law of
the Sabbath is the
chiropractic adjustment
we receive to treat spiritual
scoliosis. The sturdiest plants
that bear the best fruit are those
that have deep roots in good, rich,
nurturing soil. Sabbath school teaches
us to integrate ourselves into a loam that
is rich in art, courtesy, decency, example,
honor, music, and virtue. Its object is to
allow our spirits to grow freely beyond
narrow confines that are equivalent
to one-pint nursery containers. It
is because of its teachings that
we are able to send down our
taproots into Gospel soil,
and anchor ourselves
to the Infinite.

All who rely more on
economic security and less
on the spiritual preparedness
that is provided by observance
of the Sabbath, are more inclined
in times of crisis to grasp at straws
instead of rededicating themselves to
the proven principles that are taught on
the Sabbath. Those who put their trust in
idea gods have no-where to look for
help when the hot winds of fear
melt the foundations of their
misplaced faith in the
flavor of the
day.

If we are ever to obtain our exaltation and eternal life, we must do more than simply acknowledge that Jesus Christ is Lord. The teachings of the Sabbath makes it clear that the critical point of conversion, beyond which lie the encircling flames of fire in the Celestial Kingdom, rests in making the conscious decision to accept not only Jesus, but also to be obedient to His commandments. This includes the covenant we make with God to be observers of the Law of the Sabbath.

Sabbath day services create
a Technicolor backdrop for the
worldwide tapestry that is being
woven by the army of God, who
has been commissioned to seek
out and find the elect, and
sew them into the
fold.

Keeping in every whit
the Law of the Sabbath puts
us beyond the influence of the
adversary and endows us with the
priesthood and spiritual power that is
necessary to overcome evil, until we
have finished our work on the earth,
and obtain our exaltation.

Sabbath
day worship
helps us to break
away from limiting
beliefs. As we brush up
against the stars, we are
awakened to a new vision
that is, at first, blinding, but
as our eyes adjust to the light,
we e surprised to see, perhaps
for the first time, the world
as it really is.

Perhaps reflecting upon his Sabbath day experiences, Parley P. Pratt cried: "I have received the holy anointing, and I can never rest until the last enemy has been conquered, death destroyed, and truth reigns triumphant." His immersion in the doctrines of the kingdom had infused him with a power that would propel him in the direction of his destiny.

When we neglect
our opportunities to make
the connections that can only
be envisioned when we maintain
an eternal perspective, we neutralize
the magical capability of the Sabbath day
to raise our testimony temperature, get
our juices flowing, and stir our souls.
The Law of the Sabbath is as a human
growth hormone for our spirits.

We will not endure
for long if we rely only upon
the flickering light that is generated
by casual connections to our Heavenly
Father. He will provide an external power
source with generous and steady supplies
of dependable energy for as long as we
manifest a desire to become members
of His Second Mile Club, which is a
select group to which we have all
been invited in consequence of
our commitment to the Law
of the Sabbath.

Our Sabbath school promises direct experience with the Infinite at a spiritually charged event horizon that separates the temporal world from eternity. Nothing is taught there that would be of any interest to those who dance in the spotlight of a telestial stage. It is not an exclusive country club that is situated on a narrow ecclesiastical terrace, with membership privileges reserved only for the well-connected. "He inviteth them all to come unto him, black and white, bond and free, male and female ... and all are alike unto God, bot Jew and Gentile." (2 Nephi 26:33).

Our physical
surroundings in
the lone and dreary
world have been designed,
harsh though they may seem,
to provide a hint of familiarity.
When we are sensitive to the Spirit
as we participate in our Sabbath day
worship services, we are blessed to
establish a celestial connectivity
that permits us to click with
the heavens and commune
with the Infinite.

On the Lord's Sabbath
day, we are taught about The
Plan of Salvation in creative ways
that are alien to the understanding of
Spiritual Babylon. We attend services, to
paraphrase King Benjamin, to open our
ears, so that we might hear, and our
hearts, so that we might understand,
and our minds, that the wonders
of eternity might be unfolded,
and spread out before our
view in a breathtaking
panorama.

It is on the Sabbath that Heavenly Father is able to begin in earnest our preparation for immortality. It is then, that our eyes are really opened, our vision is perfected, and we are taught how to raise our sight so that it rests above the artificial horizons of mortality. It is then, that we steal our first fleeting look at the wonders of eternity, and realize that it is there, in heaven, where our future really lies.

As any caring
parent would, our
Father in Heaven wants
all of His children to receive
an endowment of spiritual and
priesthood power on the Sabbath,
under His roof, at His direction,
and under His guidance, for
that is our only assurance
of safe passage through
the minefields of
mortality.

On the Sabbath,
we discern the truth
behind Hamlet's euphoria:
"What a piece of work is man!
How noble in reason, how infinite
in faculty, in form and moving how
express and admirable, in action how
like an angel, in apprehension how
like a god - the beauty of the
world, the paragon of
animals!"

In an episode of "Star Trek," Q told Captain Picard: "You just don't get it, do you Jean Luc? The trial never ends. We wanted to see if you had the ability to expand your mind and your horizons. And for one brief moment you did. For that one fraction of a second, you were open to options that you had never considered. That is the exploration that awaits you. Your destiny is not mapping star systems and studying nebula, but charting the unknown possibilities of existence." To do that, none of us needs to book passage on a Galaxy Class Starship. We just need to attend our worship services on the Sabbath day, if we hope to tread upon the sanctity of space, to explore the far reaches of eternity, and to go where only a select few have ever gone before.

William W. Phelps
realized that without the
Sabbath, no-one "has found pure
space, nor seen the outside curtains,
where nothing has a place." Within the
roiling matrix of our worship, we realize
that there is no end to matter, space,
spirit, or race; virtue, might, wisdom,
or light; union, youth, priesthood,
or truth; glory, love, or being.
We begin our exploration of
eternity on the Sabbath
day.

The Law
of the Sabbath
give us the resolve
to abandon the idolatry
that is always waiting in the
wings, that it might obstruct our
vision. On the Sabbath day, we find
the ammunition we need to conquer
our self-deification. We renounce the
adoration of our own creations, as we
worship the Lord in His sanctuary. We
are liberated from a lust for power
and domination, and from
avarice, and the cult
of the state.

In spite of our focus on agency, accountability, industry, and labor, as we are exhorted to greater dedication, duty, and diligence, the truth is that nothing we can do will ever qualify us for eternal life. One of the powerful lessons we learn in Sabbath school is that of our utter dependence upon the Savior of the world for our redemption, our salvation, and our exaltation.

Without the influence of the Spirit that vitalizes the Sabbath day of the Lord, societies wither and die. They become empty shells and structures of custom and convenience, illuminated only by the flickering candlelight of superstition and magic. We need the luminosity of the Lord to be freed from bondage to our sins. The reassuring glow of the Sabbath day provides more than enough energy to light a darkened world.

As we mildly and quietly walk in the light of the Lord on a journey that will bring us to our Sabbath day worship, we are more likely to comfortably embrace the truth. As the Holy Ghost washes over us, our own spirits are "first pure, then peaceable, gentle, and easy to be entreated, full of mercy and good fruits, without partiality, and without hypocrisy." (James 3:17).

Pennies from heaven
are the only coinage that
we are permitted to carry when
we come to the Sabbath school. These
tender mercies stand in sharp contrast
to the spurious counterfeit small change
that is circulated by the money launderers,
of Satan, who lurk in the shadows, hoping
to negotiate with worshippers in a one
sided currency exchange that is
favorable only to them.

Latter-day Saints who faithfully embrace the Law of the Sabbath have discovered an important element of their spiritual revitalization. The more they contribute to the work, the greater is their happiness and joy, the more fully is God able to help them to fulfil their own destiny, and the more does the Spirit infuse them with a desire to be valiant in the cause of Zion.

Those who enjoy spiritual gifts have the image of God engraven upon their countenances. They shall ascend into the hill of the Lord, to stand in His holy place on the Sabbath, to partake of His divine nature, and all this because they have clean hands and pure hearts, and they have not lifted up their souls unto vanity, nor have they sworn deceitfully. In all things, they have kept the Lord's statutes.

The mortal
ministry of Jesus Christ
among the children of men
may be the greatest miracle of
all, but those who deny His power
that is manifest on the Sabbath day
cannot be saved on His merits alone,
simply because they have not generated
faith with enough energy to carry their
progression forward. Only a profound
attitude adjustment will jump-start
their momentum and move them
along the pathway that leads
to the Kingdom of God.

It will be
difficult for
those who have
lived a telestial
existence to justify
their behavior before
God, in the face of the
many signs and wonders He
has revealed on the Sabbath as
as both warnings and blessings.
Those of us who have witnessed
any or the least of these has seen
God moving in his majesty
and power.

Revelation may be recognized only when we have allowed ourselves to fall under the influence of the Spirit. Our acceptance of communication from the heavens waits upon our initiative. So it is in our Sabbath day worship. It is not subject to private interpretation. We simply nurture nature and then let it caper.

How fitting
when our testimony of
the Sabbath consists of our
discreet expressions relating
to the guidance we receive from
the Spirit, that is beyond our limited
understanding, and that helps us as
we face challenges, as we make
important decisions, and as we
grapple with the greatest
questions relating
to our lives.

We are intertwined
with Heavenly Father, Jesus
Christ, and with the Holy Ghost,
in palpable connections. They take
note if sparrows fall from trees, and on
cold winter nights, they help us to notice
the explosion of supernovas in distant
galaxies. They do not play dice with
Their creations; We can be sure that
They will leave nothing to chance.
Particularly when we sit in our
Sabbath day worship services,
we are at-one with Them
in every conceivable,
and unimaginable,
way.

Every time we come to Church to worship God on His holy day, it is as if it were a contemporary declaration to the world of tidings of great joy. It carries us on a groundswell of emotion that lifts us heavenward. Worship is elevated to something more dynamic than the simple mechanical observance of a multiplicity of ceremonial rules. Publishing peace on the Lord's Sabbath is the daily antidote to those negative influences that are forever attempting to canker our souls.

The Sabbath
was restored so
that latter-day Israel
might receive the Gospel
and enter into covenants of
salvation and justification, as
well as those of sanctification
and exaltation; and that by the
authority of the priesthood of
God the Sacrament might be
administered to all who
qualify by worthiness
to partake of the
emblems of
Christ.

Every time we
worthily partake of
the bread and water of the
Sacrament on the Sabbath, we are
powerfully strengthened, so that the
promises of heaven might be realized.
We invite virtue to garnish our thoughts
unceasingly. As our confidence builds,
the doctrine of the priesthood distils
upon our heads as the dews from
heaven, the Holy Ghost is our
constant companion, and its
guidance flows unto us
without compulsory
means.

On
the Lord's
Holy Day, there is
instilled within us a
sound understanding as
we search the scriptures, that
we might know the word of God.
But this is not all; we give ourselves
to prayer, and fasting, that we might
enjoy the spirit of prophecy, and the
spirit of revelation, so that when
we teach, we teach with power
and authority of God.

Our
Heavenly
Father blessed
us with the Law of
the Sabbath because He
is able to envision the worst
circumstances in which we will
find ourselves. He has preplayed,
and now we are replaying, the drama
of our lives. When He declared: "We will
prove them herewith, to see if they will
do all things whatsoever the Lord their
God shall command them," it was
as much a statement of fact as it
was a question of whether or
not we would be obedient.
(Abraham 3:25).

The Law of the Sabbath
is the spiritual equivalent
to being well-grounded. It is
a powerful positive motivator. We
remember Nephi, who described those
who were "pressing forward, and they came
forth and caught hold of the end of the Rod
of Iron; and they did press forward through
the mist of darkness, clinging to the Rod
of Iron, even until they did come forth
and partake of the fruit of the tree."
(1 Nephi 8:24).

"For behold, it is as easy to give heed to the word of Christ," that we hear on the Sabbath day of the Lord, which will point to us "a straight course to eternal bliss, as it was for our fathers to give heed to this compass, which would point unto them a straight course to the promised land." (Alma 37: 44). As it was for Alma and his people, so it is for us today. Christ is our Navigator. He is our Liahona. If we will follow Him, even through the tornados of life, we will discover that no wind can blow except it fills our sails.

Joseph Smith taught:
"We may profit by noticing the first intimation of the spirit of revelation; for instance, when we feel pure intelligence flowing into us, it may give us sudden strokes of ideas ... By learning the Spirit of God and understanding it, we may grow into the principle of revelation." The Sabbath day, then, is a schoolmaster that is designed to bring us, by that same spirit of insight, intuition, inspiration and revelation, to the doctrine of our Lord Jesus Christ.

We
honor the
Sabbath day at the
start of a week that is
sure to have its ups and
downs. In our obedience,
there is consistency. It provides
a bastion of stability in the midst
of the turmoil of the world. It has
a powerful and influential capacity
to center our hearts, might, mind,
and strength on our covenant
relationship with Heavenly
Father, Jesus Christ,
and the Holy
Ghost.

From the bosom of eternity,
something needed to be done that
would counteract the unforgiving reality
check of our birth. To that end, our Father
has instilled within us the instinctive desire to
enjoy bonds with each other that can transcend
physical relationships. Our hearts are stamped with
a blueprint for our survival, that of His intuitive
instruction, the insight we will need to properly
organize ourselves and prepare every needful
thing, so that on the Sabbath day of the Lord
we might establish a house of prayer, and
of fasting, faith, learning, glory, and
order; even a house of God, where
dreams come true, and where
eternal relationships are not
only magical, but also
wondrously possible.

When we have been
privileged to reach out
and touch the face of God,
as we do during our Sabbath day
services, the Spirit that is present can
be augmented by the medium of music.
Even before the foundations of the earth
were laid, a celestial harmony floated
in the air, when "the morning stars
sang together, and all the sons
of God shouted for joy."
(Job 38:7).

As
we ponder
the Sabbath day,
let us remember that
the Savior is our life-line,
providing security when our
footing is unsure and the foaming
sea is streaming across our deck. He is
our compass, showing us the way, especially
when the course before us is unclear. He is our
chart that warns us of hidden dangers, and our
barometer, alerting us to impending storms. He
is our lookout, standing as our sentinel when
we are distracted by trivial concerns, and He
holds the line that trails in our wake, and
offers safety should we lose our footing
and fall overboard. He is the wind
that fills our sails, that we may
find our way home.

One of the blessings of the Sabbath day is that it may inflict upon us a benevolent blindness that actually helps us to see more clearly than those with 20:20 vision. Those who keep the holy day of the Lord, feel with a vibrancy that is incorporeal and indefinable. It can kindle a light within their hearts that overshadows the somatic senses, and that is more valuable than precious jewels.

Our active engagement with the Sabbath day helps us to see things as they really are, and at the same time, it compels us to be benevolently blind to the shortcomings of others. Just so, Heavenly Father is blind to our own failures when we come to our Sabbath day services having already completed the arduous process of repentance.

On the Sabbath day, as before the holy altars in the temple, we make sacred covenants with the Lord, the fulfillment of which will bring us earthly blessings and eternal exaltation. As we focus our attention on obeying His commandments and being worthy to partake of the Sacrament and to attend the temple, our thirst will be quenched with the living water provided by the Gospel of Jesus Christ.

Putting His children
under covenant to obey the
Law of the Sabbath must surely
be the prototypical example of the
absolute genius behind God's Plan of
Salvation, as it focuses our minds and
our spirits on our covenants, the Savior,
His Atonement, and on the commandments.
That discipline expands the capacity of
our understanding, and allows us to
experience how a Gospel-centered
lifestyle can be greater than
the sum of its parts.

On the Sabbath, we
are taught to engage
the gears of the engine
that drives us toward the
achievement of our goals. It
prevents us from remaining at a
stand-still with our transmissions
idling in neutral, and being left
to wonder why we are not being
magically propelled forward
with no effort on our
own part.

The Sabbath is
a scale that measures the
strength of our integrity and of
our discipleship. It is a barometer
that illustrates how spirituality can be
inseparably interwoven into our character.
It beckons us to pattern our lives after
the example of the Savior, that we
might internalize the principles
of the Gospel, and remember
our priesthood covenants.

On the Sabbath day, as we turn our attention to the scriptures, to fasting, to prayer, to the Sacrament, and to an active discipline-based lifestyle, we are more likely to make progress as we follow the Rod of Iron toward the Tree of Life. If we falter in our faith during the journey, we remember the word of the Lord to Israel: "I will heal their backsliding, I will "love them freely: for mine anger is turned away." (Hosea 14:4).

How we embrace
the Sabbath day determines
how we handle our weaknesses,
our imperfections, and sin. Without
it, our self-defeating behaviors always
threaten to impede our progress. Because
the covenant of the Sacrament establishes
a partnership with our Heavenly Father, the
Savior, and the Holy Ghost, we can turn
the tables on Satan, and actually use
our inadequacies, blemishes, and
even our transgressions, as our
own personal stepping-stones
to higher achievement.

Perhaps it is because it is so easy to get out of focus, lose our grip on the Iron Rod, and wander from strict obedience, to the neglect of our covenants, that we are commanded to regularly and repetitively participate in our worship services on the Sabbath. As we do so every week, it is not so much vain repetition as it is God's theatrical encore.

Those who
decline the offer
of the riches of eternity
that might have been unfolded
to their view through the Law of
the Sabbath day are doomed to eke
out a subsistence level of existence in
scarcity of their basic spiritual needs.
With the smorgasbord of life spread
out before them, they settle for the
processed factory food that is
dished out by the automats
of the world. They live
beneath the poverty
level, and are not
even aware
of it.

When we worship with others on the Sabbath day, the doctrines of the kingdom, or the solemnities of eternity, are positioned right in the forefront of our conscious awareness. We take our understanding as far as our capacity allows us to go, because it is tailored to suit our individual circumstances, and yet it is collectively understood and is universally applicable.

As long as we
have listened to the voice of
the Lord, our comprehension of the
Law of the Sabbath will flow easily and
poetically to our minds. Our persistence
and our participation will lead to practiced
fluency with the language of the Spirit that is
the result of the inspiration that will come as
we approach the Sabbath day with faith, fasting,
and prayer. As our minds are enlightened, we
will be cast off into a stream of revelation
and carried along in the quickening
currents of direct experience
with the mind and
will of God.

It is during our journey of faith on the Sabbath, that we begin to really appreciate the power of our position, that we might one day "flourish in immortal youth, unhurt amidst the war of elements, the wreck of matter, and the crash of worlds." (Joseph Addison).

When
we seek
to understand
ourselves from the
eternal perspective of
the Sabbath, we raise our
sights to the possibility of
an expanded view of life. We
are up and moving on the
pathway to our personal
rediscovery and self
actualization.

It is said that
time is the fire in
which we burn. This may
be true, in the sense that it is
by fire and the Holy Ghost that
time becomes the element within
which we work out our salvation
with fear and trembling before
the Lord, on the holy
Sabbath day.

The defining
characteristics of
the society of Saints
that are displayed for
all to see on the Sabbath
day are simply the result of
a spiritual transformation that
occurs when its members live,
to the best of their ability,
the celestial law of our
Lord and Savior.

It
is on the
Sabbath that
we learn that it
rains pennies from
heaven. This celestial
coinage was the first to
bear the inscription "In God
We Trust." His legal tender is
date sensitive, and it regains
its greatest value one day
each week, on the holy
day of the Lord.

The Law of the Sabbath allows us to exercise our eye of faith. The sum of that experience establishes sure footing on the bedrock of unchanging principles that are taught without ambiguity in Sabbath day school.

On the Sabbath, we open our minds to options we have never considered, envisioning a special place called Kolob, signifying the first creation that is the closest body to the celestial, or to the residence of God.

In one of the more memorable episodes of "Star Trek," Captain Picard asks Q: "What is it you're trying to tell me?" To which, the omnipotent and omniscient Q tantalizingly replies: "You'll find out!" So it is in on the Sabbath day.

We flee from Spiritual Babylon and let the Law of the Sabbath rule supreme in our lives. We learn about the process by which we may be purified from the effects of sin. This occurs when the Sabbath drives the law into our inward parts.

Surely, we need
the wise counsel of
the Spirit now, as much
as we ever have, because we
have exponentially increased
the odds that we will destroy
ourselves if we are careless;
if we do not both carefully
and prayerfully obey the
Law of the Sabbath.

We engage
the Sabbath day,
that we might learn to
abide by the laws of heaven,
even as we tarry upon the earth.
We yearn for our hearts to burn
within us, and for the Spirit to
speak to us, so that it might
open up the scriptures to
our understanding.

Our observances
on the Sabbath day trigger
a cleansing. The process of
of sanctification through the
Atonement allows us to approach
God's throne with confidence that
He will grant us the blessings we
need, rather than those we
only thought we had
wanted.

Each week, on the Sabbath day, the priesthood of God draws upon His grace, allowing us to receive blessings by binding us to Him thru revelation by the means of a covenant of action. Because Heavenly Father honors the principle of free will, our progression patiently waits upon our initiative. The Gospel will force none of us to heaven.

The Sabbath
stands ready to
guide us unerringly,
that we might know for
ourselves the truthfulness
of all things. Even more, as
it molds us and shapes us in
to new creatures in Christ, pure
intelligence, or the knowledge of
God, will freely flow unto our
minds and our spirits, as the
dews of Carmel.

Truly, when God said: "Let there be light," it was a simple statement of fact as much as it was a command. It was an invitation to recognize, embrace, and celebrate the light dancing all around us on the Sabbath, as in a revelatory rapture.

As we participate in devotion services on the Sabbath day, we become like our Father in Heaven. The repetition in our worship nurtures spiritual growth; its reiteration encourages us to be even more obedient, that we might more faithfully follow the Savior's example. We realize that our finest hours are those when unanticipated challenge is met with extraordinary response. We invest those hours in the Sabbath day, to insulate us from the snares of Satan that exist to steal from us that which is most precious, that is our spiritual identity as God's children.

It will
not be easy
for those who
have turned their
backs on the Sabbath,
who no longer will allow
Christ into their lives, to be
saved in the Kingdom of God.
They are slow to learn that it was
thru the Atonement that our Father
in Heaven links the righteous efforts
of all of His children to those of His
Firstborn Son, to bring to pass His
great and eternal purposes.

We remember the Sabbath, to keep it holy, because we want to be redeemed of God; to be numbered among those who will participate in the first resurrection. We clear our minds to focus on eternity, against the backdrop of the everyday world to which all of us will physically return each time we leave the house of worship.

One of the articles of faith of The Church of Jesus Christ of Latter-day Saints is that its members believe that The Plan of God provides us with institutional and personal continuing revelation that comes from Heavenly Father through the medium of the Holy Ghost. If, during our Sabbath day worship services, however, we keep looking for the spectacular, we might just overlook the steady stream of revealed communication that cascades down from above.

As we honor
the Sabbath, precious
emanations of familiar
and soothing oscillations
of energy will resonate from
within the limitless reserves of the
Spirit. These are selflessly shared by
the One who has promised to carry us
along on rolling waves of revelation
toward a shoreline of stability that
nurtures a more sure witness of
the Savior's divinity, no matter
what the tide may bring
in tomorrow.

About The Author

Phil Hudson and his wife Jan have 7 children and over 25 grandchildren. They enjoy spending time with their family at their cabin nestled in the Selkirk Mountains, on the shore of Priest Lake, the crown jewel of North Idaho. Phil had a successful dental practice in Spokane, Washington for 43 years, before retiring in 2015. He has an eclectic mix of hobbies, and enjoys the out of doors. He always finds time, however, to record his thoughts on his laptop, and understands Isaac Asimov's response when he was asked: If you knew that you had only 10 minutes left to live, what would you do?" He answered: "I'd type faster."

Phil received the inspiration to write this book while he and Jan were serving as missionaries for The Church of Jesus Christ of Latter-day Saints, in the Kingdom of Tonga. While there, they celebrated their 50th wedding anniversary.

It is in our worship on the Sabbath that our Heavenly Father has provided a way for us to return to the secret garden of our childhood, that we might fully mature. As Wordsworth wrote: "Heaven lies about us in our infancy. Shades of the prison house begin to close upon the growing boy, but he beholds the light and whence it flows. He sees it in his joy. The youth, who daily farther from the east must travel, still is nature's priest, and by the vision splendid, is on his way attended. At length the man perceives it die away, and fade into the light of common day."

By The Author

Essays

    Volume One: Spray From The Ocean Of Thought
    Volume Two: Ripples On A Pond
    Volume Three: Serendipitous Meanderings
    Volume Four: Presents Of Mind
    Volume Five: Mental Floss
    Volume Six: Fitness Training For The Mind And Spirit

First Principles and Ordinances Series

    Faith - Our Hearts Are Changed
    Repentance - A Broken Heart and a Contrite Spirit
    Baptism - One Hundred And One Reasons Why We Are Baptized
    The Holy Ghost - That We Might Have His Spirit To Be With Us
    The Sacrament - This Do In Remembrance Of Me

Book of Mormon Commentary

    Volume One: Born In The Wilderness
    Volume Two: Voices From The Dust
    Volume Three: Journey To Cumorah

Doctrine & Covenants Commentary

    Volume One - Sections 1 - 34
    Volume Two - Sections 35 - 57

Minute Musings: Spontaneous Combustions of Thought

    Volume One
    Volume Two
    Volume Three

Calendars:

    In His Own Words: Discovering William Tyndale
    As I Think About The Savior
    Scriptural Symbols

Children's Books

    Muddy, Muddy
    The Thirteen Articles of Faith
    Happy Birthday

Doctrinal Themes

    The House of the Lord

A Thought For Each Day of the Year

    Faith
    Repentance
    Baptism
    The Holy Ghost
    The Sacrament
    The House of the Lord
    The Plan of Salvation
    The Atonement
    Revelation
    The Sabbath
    Life's Greatest Questions

Professional Publications

    Diode Laser Soft Tissue Surgery Volume One
    Diode Laser Soft Tissue Surgery Volume Two
    Diode Laser Soft Tissue Surgery Volume Three

These, and other titles, are available from online retailers.

On the
Sabbath day, the
power of godliness is
unmistakable. And without
the authority of the priesthood
that administers the ordinances,
the power of godliness is not
manifest, even unto those
who profess to know
Jesus Christ on
every other
level.

Quid magis possum dicere?

www.ingramcontent.com/pod-product-compliance
Lightning Source LLC
Chambersburg PA
CBHW060508240426
43661CB00007B/954